The Word Detective

The **WORD** Detective

by Evan Morris

ALGONQUIN BOOKS
OF CHAPEL HILL

Published by

Algonquin Books of Chapel Hill

Post Office Box 2225

Chapel Hill, North Carolina 27515-2225

a division of

Workman Publishing

708 Broadway

New York, New York 10003

Printed in the United States of America.

Published simultaneously in Canada

  by Thomas Allen & Son Limited.

Design by Anne Winslow.

Spot illustrations by Carl Wiens.

ISBN 1-56512-239-9

To my parents,

William and Mary Davis Morris,

Who taught me to love words,

And to my brother,

John Boyd Morris,

1938–1999,

whose humor, decency, and courage

live in the hearts of

all who knew him.

ACKNOWLEDGMENTS

I wish to thank, first and foremost, the faithful readers of my column, without whose support and encouragement the present book would not exist and I would probably be selling time shares in Arkansas over the Internet. I would also like to thank the newspapers that carry my column, even the one that edits out all the funny stuff before printing it. I'm sure it has its reasons.

I would also like to thank my wife, Kathy Wollard, and my agent, Janis Donnaud, for their encouragement, persistence, and good advice; my son, Aaron; and my editor, Amy Gash, and all the folks at Algonquin for shepherding this book into print.

Thanks are also due to all my friends at Skadden, Arps, without whose support and encouragement I would still be working there, and (in no particular order) to Barry Popik, Susan Davis, Jeff Coleman, Lynn Kotula, Dan Poor, John Guthrie, Jim Vincent, Jesse Sheidlower, William Safire, Susan Cox, Debra Solomon, James Himber, Pete Hamill, Rick Freyer, Nancy Hoffman, Vincent Siino, Steven Stark, all my siblings, all my in-laws in Ohio, Terry O'Connor, Becky Lorberfeld, Ray-Bari Pizza, Jill Cornell, Benjamin Wheeler, the nice folks at Zingone Grocers on Columbus Avenue, Mark Wall, Susie Day, Eloise Eisenhardt, Jon Rosenblatt, Spencer Beckwith, Frank Pike, Dave Hill, Jon Bassewitz, Esteban Chalbaud, Dan Dial, the *New York Daily News,* Reg Gale, Tony Marro, Libby Colahan, Mike Morris, Jane Baum, Sonia Dinham, Marjorie Zaik, Fran Wood, Jonathan Powell, Lee Morrow, the American Dialect Society, Brownie, Pokey, Ernie, Rufus, Fang, and Puff, and anyone who ever laughed at my joke about the penguins in the convertible.

INTRODUCTION

It all started with sticky dimes. It was 1958, I was eight years old, and my older sister and I sat in the library of my family's home in suburban Connecticut, opening the dozen or so envelopes that had arrived in the day's mail. Each envelope contained ten cents in some form—usually dimes or nickels taped securely to small pieces of cardboard, but sometimes a hodgepodge of stamps—and it was our job to extract the loot and sort it dutifully into plastic salad bowls. A grown-up would probably have regarded our task as tedious, but we, innocent of child labor laws, had begged our parents to let us open the letters.

In my eight-year-old world, encountering just one letter containing actual money would have been a memorable event.

A pile of such magic envelopes was a postal miracle that boggled my small mind, on a par with having the tooth fairy drop by for dinner. As a matter of fact, I was beginning to have my doubts about the tooth fairy's existence, but here was solid evidence of a mail fairy out there somewhere with an apparently inexhaustible supply of sticky dimes.

To my parents, however, the dimes were simply the fruits of a good idea. My father was editor in chief of Grosset & Dunlap, a large publishing firm in New York City. Several years earlier he had begun writing a syndicated newspaper column called "Words, Wit and Wisdom," answering readers' questions about word origins and language usage, and he had learned several useful things about his readers from the questions they sent in. His readers were very insecure about the size of their vocabularies, they were similarly worried about making grammatical errors, and they were fascinated and often mystified by "teen" slang. My parents' good idea was to produce simple, helpful pamphlets on each of these topics and market them through my father's column for ten cents each. The response from readers was phenomenal, and soon my sister and I were stuffing envelopes with copies of *The Morris Self-Scoring Home Vocabulary Test,* a hipster glossary called *The Real Gone Lexicon,* and similar creations.

I was aware of my father's vocation, of course, although I tended to view his profession through the pragmatic prism of a young boy's interests. I was oblivious to the fact that Grosset published some of the most popular novels of the 1950s, but I was thrilled that my father apparently possessed the keys to a bottomless trove of the Hardy Boys, Steve Canyon, and Tom Swift Jr. books I loved.

My parents encouraged all their children to read, and I watched relatively little television as a child. The problem my parents faced was not in getting us to read, but in getting us to stop. "No reading at the dinner table" was a frequent admonition, which we quietly subverted by memorizing the ingredients list of every condiment on the table. My sister and I argued over first crack at each new *Life, Look,* or *Newsweek* that arrived in the mail, and I spent many an afternoon driving my mother to distraction by following her from room to room begging her to explain the notoriously oblique cartoons in the *New Yorker* to me.

By the 1960s, my parents had branched out into writing books, creating a series of reference works that included *It's Easy to Increase Your Vocabulary* and *The Harper Dictionary of Contemporary Usage* and culminated in the popular *Morris Dictionary of Word and Phrase Origins*. My father had accepted the position of editor in chief of the *American Heritage Dictionary,* an ambitious project that would, after nearly ten years, result in a dictionary that many authorities today regard as a revolutionary leap in American lexicography.

While my father was at the office during the week, my mother labored at home over stacks of manuscript pages. On the weekends, my father would rise by seven at the latest to work on his columns for the coming week, and I awoke each Saturday morning to the sound of his ancient Royal upright manual typewriter pounding away downstairs like thunder in the distance (although not quite distant enough to sleep through). By the time I graduated from high school, our second-floor library/ guest bedroom had been turned into a full-time office buried under stacks of manuscripts and reference materials, and when I headed off to college, my parents quickly filled my old bedroom with files, boxes of correspondence, and spare encyclopedias. By the early 1980s, my parents were both working at home, churning out six newspaper columns every week as well as producing books on English usage and word origins.

Then suddenly, in 1986, my mother died, leaving my father to carry on alone. Given the circumstances, my father carried on quite well, continuing to write his newspaper column and maintaining an active social and professional life, traveling abroad, and making new friends.

By the early 1990s, however, my father had understandably tired of writing a daily newspaper column for more than thirty-five years. He announced his intention to retire his column at the dinner table one Sunday afternoon when most of his children, now grown and with families and careers of their own, happened to be present. "Words, Wit and Wisdom," he declared, was kaput. "Unless," he added, in what had become a very quiet room, "one of you is interested in writing it."

I don't think my father actually expected any one of us to take him up on his offer. All three of my sisters had done editorial work on my parents' books, and all six of us had long become accustomed to being tapped as sources for current slang. But none of us had ever, to my knowledge, entertained the thought of stepping into our parents' professional shoes. To me, certainly, the very expertise and erudition that had made my father successful and famous also precluded any such fantasies on my part. My father had worked with H. L. Mencken, had been a professional lexicographer for fifty years, and counted among his friends a constellation of intellectual luminaries. So I was as surprised as anyone at the table when, in the awkward silence that followed my father's momentous announcement, I heard myself say, "I'll give it a shot," ignoring the voice in the back of my head shouting, "Whaddayou, nuts or something? You can't write a daily newspaper column!" Almost as soon as I opened my mouth, I began to wish I'd kept it shut, but it was too late.

I spent the next few months poring over stacks of my parents' back columns and studying books on word origins and the evolution of English, and in the process I made two important discoveries: first, that I was absolutely fascinated by the subject itself, and second, that I knew much more about the English language than I had thought I did. The combination of my own grounding in English, my somewhat dusty but sound grasp of Latin, and more than thirty years of incidental linguistic knowledge gleaned from my parents via dinner table osmosis, combined to allay my initial terror at the thought of writing about etymology. My father and I worked out a collaborative arrangement that allowed me to write one or two columns per week, which he would then review and tune up, if necessary, before tossing them into the mix with his own columns. To my surprise, my father did very little fiddling with my writing, and "Words, Wit and Wisdom" soon began appearing in newspapers around the world under the byline of William and Evan Morris.

Almost as soon as I began writing the column with my father, I discovered that I was far from being alone in my fascination with the stories behind words. Mentioning the column in casual conversation with nearly anyone, from my dentist to the proprietor of the corner newsstand, would be certain to elicit either a favorite word-origin story to share or a question about an obscure term that had been simmering unanswered in the back of that person's mind for years.

Early on in my apprenticeship, I came across a series of word-origin books by the poet and lexicographer John Ciardi (*A Browser's Dictionary, A Second Browser's Dictionary,* and *Good Words to You,* now all, sadly, out of print). The more words I traced back through time for our readers, the more I appreciated Ciardi's observation that each word, no matter how humble, was "a small fossil poem written by the race itself." The evolution of words, in many ways, is an organic process akin to the evolution of animal and plant species. Words grow and prosper for a time, often spawning new words, but eventually they age and in many cases even become extinct. Now that English is in many senses a global language, words travel from country to country and mutate in both their forms and meanings, often changing their connotations entirely or combining in idiomatic uses that would have struck listeners just a century earlier as nonsensical. I would not, for instance, wish to be the one to try to explain *rock and roll* or *pushing the envelope* to Noah Webster.

Words don't do all this on their own, of course. The words and language we speak today are the product (more a work in progress, actually) of an enormous committee consisting of nearly every person who ever lived; most of these people never spoke our modern English, and it shows. If our words, metaphors, and idioms sometimes make no sense to a logical mind, or if it seems as though there ought to be a happy *gruntled* to accompany the cranky *disgruntled,* we have only ourselves to blame. (There actually used to be a *gruntled,* but it meant "grunting like a pig" or "cranky," and it faded away as *disgruntled,* which simply added the intensifier *dis-* and meant exactly the same thing, became popular.)

The good news about our unruly, intensely democratic way of making and using words is that the lack of any central planning and administration authority, the absence of a Ministry of Proper English, makes our language one of the most energetic, flexible, and just plain fun tongues on earth. This vitality and unpredictability of English as it is actually spoken drives the prissy Language Cops of the world absolutely bananas, of course, but it warms the cockles of any true word lover's heart.

Soon after I began writing the column, I discovered that I possessed another tool that would prove immensely valuable in untangling the histories of words and phrases: a healthy skepticism. Many of the questions my father and I received from readers asked about the truth of a story the reader had heard about the origin of a word or phrase. Was *cop* actually an acronym for *constable on patrol?* Did *hooker* really spring from the fondness of Civil War general Joseph Hooker and his men for camp followers? (The answer is a resounding no in both cases.) I quickly came to regard every "remarkable" word-origin story I encountered with the jaundiced eye and prove-it-buddy attitude I had honed on the streets of New York City, and I was rarely disappointed in my quest for linguistic balderdash to debunk. One of the lessons I have learned over the past decade is that the more interesting or heartwarming or unusual or "cool" a word-origin story is, the less likely it is to reside in the same ballpark as the truth. And I have learned the hard way that entertaining but unsubstantiated etymologies have a distressing tendency to make their way into print, so I do my best never to accept and promulgate popular word stories without making darn sure that I either solidly verify them or label them as only possibilities.

Unfortunately, my determination not to endorse etymological fables has sometimes been distressingly at odds with the apparent prevailing public desire to believe all sorts of nonsense about word origins, and some of my readers are not shy about making their wishes, and delusions, quite clear. "You say that the origin of *the whole nine yards* is unknown," goes a typical letter of a certain sort, "but some simple research conducted even by a boob such as yourself would reveal that the phrase was invented by my uncle Floyd in 1957, when he successfully escaped from a Venusian spacecraft using a ladder exactly nine yards long constructed from dental floss. Somewhere in my attic I have a letter from Ed Sullivan confirming this fact. Why won't you print the truth?"

Occasionally an especially emphatic reader letter prompts me to reconsider my decision, years ago, not to pursue my first career choice, dog grooming. "Your claim that the word *thug* originally came from *thuggee,* ritual strangulation and robbery supposedly practiced by followers of the Hindu goddess Kali (whom you describe as possessing 'huge glowing red eyes, fangs, and a necklace of human skulls'), is ridiculous," wrote one reader a few years ago, who then went on to helpfully inform me that "the many modern followers of the great goddess Kali have no use for the slanderous antics of mouth-breathing morons like you. I'd be careful whose goddess you offend, especially since Kali liked to drink the blood of her opponents in battle! Be warned: we are not amused." After I emerged a few weeks later from meditating on this letter in my coat closet, I spent the next several months checking for glowing red eyes on every subway train I boarded. Eventually I concluded that it was impossible to distinguish between disgruntled Kali fans and disgruntled Mets fans, so I gradually relaxed. I recalled that my father had spawned similar outrage in the mid-1960s when he dared to suggest in print that Ringo Starr was not exactly the world's greatest drummer, a parallel that comforted me (although the bit about Kali drinking the blood of her enemies seemed a bit more serious than the wrath of a few thousand irate Beatles fans).

After a few weeks of laboriously hunting-and-pecking my columns on an old Underwood manual typewriter, I reluctantly broke down, dipped my bruised digits into my bank account, and bought my first computer. Within a few months I was collecting the columns I wrote for newspapers into a bimonthly illustrated newsletter, which I offered to readers for the princely sum of ten dollars per year, an amount scientifically calculated to land me in the poorhouse as quickly as possible. In considering possible names for my new project, I decided to recycle the name of a radio program my father had produced years earlier, *The Word Detective.* (This name seemed so appropriate, in fact, that in 1996 I also changed the name of my newspaper column from "Words, Wit and Wisdom" to "The Word Detective.")

The Word Detective newsletter was an immediate success with its hundreds of subscribers, but each month saw an increasing number of copies returned to me in small plastic bags after having been stomped, shredded, and often apparently chewed in transit by unknown parties. Just as I was about to throw in the towel, however, the Internet arrived to save my bacon.

Early 1995 saw the debut of *The Word Detective on the Web* (www.word-detective.com), a site where readers could browse current and past columns and, more important, send in their questions via e-mail. Over the past five years, readership of the Web *Word Detective* has jumped from dozens to thousands per week, and the site has been the recipient of numerous prestigious (but inexplicably cash-free) awards. And while the column "The Word Detective" currently appears in newspapers all over the United States, as well as in Mexico and Japan, the growing popularity of the Internet has broadened its global audience by millions of readers, from small towns in Iowa to small towns in China. Reader mail, the real index of any columnist's success, currently runs about five hundred questions per week.

Approximately one hundred of those questions are really one particular question, about perhaps the most obnoxious riddle ever invented: "There are three common words in the English language that end with *gry. Angry* is one and *hungry* is another. What is the third word? Everyone uses it every day and everyone knows what it means. If you have been listening, I have already told you what the word is."

When I received this question for the first time about four years ago, I spent a good deal of time trying to figure out the answer and, after pounding my head against the wall for a week or two, did some serious research and arrived at the following realizations: first, we can all stop looking for that third *gry* word. There is no other "common English word" ending in *gry,* although there are a few obscure ones, such as *aggry* (a type of bead) and *gry* itself (meaning "a very small amount").

Second, no word ending in *gry* was ever the proper answer to this insipid, annoying riddle. The wording of the riddle itself has been badly mangled as it was passed from person to person over the years, but the original form was evidently a trick question (as many riddles are) that used double-talk to send the listener off on a wild-goose chase looking for a third *gry* word. Depending on the form of the riddle, the proper answer may actually have been *it, language,* or some other tricky answer. No one knows for sure because the original form of the riddle has long since been lost in the mists of time, rendering the whole mess unsolvable. Trying to untangle the *gry* riddle today is right up there on the Pointlessness Scale with deconstructing the *Sergeant Pepper* album cover or assessing the structural dynamics of Donald Trump's hairdo. No one knows, no one will ever know, so please get over it.

I explained all this to my readers, of course. Still the letters and e-mails came by the bucketful pleading for "the third *gry* word." I explained it all again and even wrote a long essay on the subject, which I posted on my Web page. And still every morning brought a fresh crop of dozens of earnest *gry* queries. By now I was getting cranky. (Correction: I was already cranky. I was becoming homicidal.) I created a giant flashing chartreuse banner for my Web page that warned visitors that all further *gry* seekers would have their names forwarded directly to a group of crazed Kali cultists I happened to know. It didn't work, of course; nothing does, and I have finally given up. This *gry* business will outlast us all, a fact that, while depressing, did supply me with a good idea for the inscription on my tombstone: "There are three words ending in *gry: angry, hungry,* and? . . . Wake me up, and I'll tell you the third."

Most questions I receive, thankfully, have nothing to do with *gry* and often provide entertaining (and occasionally disquieting) insight into who actually reads my column. I am approached, for instance, to settle an inordinate number of drunken "bar bets" born in taverns all over the world, as well as arguments between husbands and wives or workers and their bosses, situations requiring the sort of delicacy and tact I would have thought it amply evident that I lack. Luckily, so far I know of only one divorce in which my column can fairly be said to have been a causative factor.

Many letters come from young people impertinently questioning the sanity of a grandparent who uses antiquated phrases such as *mean as gar broth* (an apparently vile soup made from the apparently vile garfish) or plaintively begging for help with their homework. To such academically delinquent pleas, usually sent late on Sunday nights, I turn a righteously deaf ear, pointing the wayward youngsters toward their school libraries (probably thus ensuring myself at least one more generation of disgruntled Kali worshipers).

By far the largest category of questions I receive are those that arrive during the workday from office workers who are, to put it bluntly, wasting eons of company time arguing among themselves about the origin of *dead as a doornail* or the logic of "Feed a cold, starve a fever." If no one answers when you call customer service for your computer, or your accountant puts you on hold for twenty minutes, or the telephone company service rep seems to be arguing with a co-worker while you try to explain that you did not call Tahiti for forty-five minutes on New Year's Eve, there's a pretty good chance that my column is ultimately to blame. The easy access to the Internet many companies inexplicably grant their employees (what's next? cable TV on every desk?) has apparently made my Web site a major factor in the declining productivity of workers all over the world.

Not bad for a newspaper column that began way back in 1954. Sadly, my father died in January 1994, too soon to see the new direction his creation had taken, but gratified, I am sure, by the knowledge that his work would continue. For my part, I am deeply grateful to my father for my apprenticeship, and to both my father and mother for investing me with the ability to continue the column on my own. That this book is dedicated to my parents is no mere formality. To them I owe everything that I have accomplished and may, in the future, dream to do.

N O T E : In the summer of 1998, after twenty years of living in New York City, my wife and I bought an 1870 farmhouse in rural Ohio. Predictably, we could not completely forsake life in the Big Apple and consequently now spend most of our time shuttling back and forth between Manhattan and Ohio. I suspect that my true legal address lies somewhere near Breezewood on the Pennsylvania Turnpike. Aside from the Capraesque charm of our little saga (I snatch a moment to work on the screenplay, in fact, every time we stop for gas), my peripatetic existence is relevant to readers of this book because some of the contents were written in, and refer to life in, New York City, while other parts (the parts with cows) were clearly written in Ohio. My publisher, who has only your best interests at heart, feels that you, the reader, would be deeply confused and disturbed, possibly to the point of demanding a refund, if I did not explain this. If, however, you are just browsing and haven't yet bought this book, you can probably safely disregard the whole matter.

The Word Detective

amok

Q: A magazine article I read recently described a baby-sitter as being unfit because she allowed the children in her care to "run amuck," which immediately made me wonder about that phrase. Any clues?

—Doris S., Toledo, Ohio.

Do you mean "any clues to where the children went"? I'd check the coat closet, personally. If they're not there, they're probably in the cupboard under the kitchen sink. I used to be very good at eluding my baby-sitter for hours at a time, or at least until she forgot about my feeding an entire jar of grape jam to the dog. I think the reason I don't remember any of my baby-sitters very clearly is probably that I met each of them only once.

Still, as trying as I may have been to my baby-sitters, I never actually ran amuck in the original sense of the word, and I doubt that the children in that magazine article did, either. *Amuck,* more properly spelled *amok,* comes from the Malay word *amok,* meaning "a state of murderous frenzy." In English, the word *amok* dates back to the sixteenth century and the first contacts between Europeans and the inhabitants of Malaysia. The standard story of the word is that the Malays were (as one European account of the period put it) "susceptible to bouts of

AMOK comes from the Malay word meaning "a state of murderous frenzy."

depression and drug use," which then led them to engage in murderous rampages. Anyone in the path of the person running amok, it was said, was likely to be sliced and diced with a particularly nasty native sword known as a *kris*.

One need not be overly politically correct to suspect that accounts of the *amok* phenomenon reported by Europeans may have been somewhat melodramatic and culturally biased. Nonetheless, *amok* entered English with the general meaning of "murderous frenzy" and was usually applied to animals, such as elephants, who attacked humans in the course of a rampage.

As is often the case, however, the meaning of the phrase in English was gradually diluted over the next few centuries until *running amok* became a metaphor used to describe someone who was simply out of control in some respect, and not necessarily chopping folks up. Still, you'll never catch me baby-sitting.

armed to the teeth

Q: Could you explain *armed to the teeth,* please? I remember reading this expression in a translation of the *Odyssey.* Does it refer to some form of armor that ran all the way to the gum and chopper region? Or does it mean that a warrior was so well fortified with weapons that he also held a knife or something in his mouth?

—*Paul S., St. Louis, Missouri.*

EVAN MORRIS

Until I did some research, I had always assumed that *armed to the teeth* had something to do with the knife-in-mouth school of personal armament. Like many folks, I have a dim childhood memory, gleaned from old pirate movies, of buccaneers swinging aboard a captured ship, brandishing blunderbusses in both hands, cutlasses clenched in their teeth. I don't think I can adequately convey how thrillingly illicit those images seemed to me at the time, but keep in mind that I was living in an age when one of the worst things a child could do was to run while holding a pair of scissors. Swinging on a rope while holding a sword in your mouth? Cool! No wonder those guys all wore eye patches.

But it turns out that *armed to the teeth* is just one of many uses of the phrase *to the teeth,* meaning "very fully" or "completely." *To the teeth* has been used as an equivalent for the popular *up to here* (with hand signal indicating the neck region) for quite a long time, since around the fourteenth century. You could, it seems, just as well be fed to the teeth, if you had eaten a large meal, or even, if sufficiently exasperated, be fed up to the teeth (at which point you might arm yourself to the teeth, I suppose).

> It turns out that ARMED TO THE TEETH is just one of many uses of the phrase *to the teeth,* meaning "very fully" or "completely."

The first modern use of *armed to the teeth* was in an 1849 speech by the English industrialist and statesman Richard Cobden, who, speaking of his nation's defense budget, asked, "Is there any reason why we should be armed to the teeth?" He obviously hadn't been watching enough pirate movies.

bar

Q: My girlfriend asked me what I thought were the origins of the terms *bar exam* and *passing the bar.* After looking up *bar* to find that one definition of the word is "the railing in a courtroom that encloses the place about the judge where prisoners are stationed or where the business of the court is transacted in civil cases," I surmised that *passing the bar* referred to entering the court of law or, rather, being considered fit to enter the court of law by passing a bar examination. She, of course, disagrees, and she insists that this *bar* has something to do with *raising the bar,* that is, to allow entrance. Can you help?

—*Andrew W., via the Internet.*

Honestly, I don't know what gets into you folks sometimes. Any fan of Davy Crockett knows that *bar* is simply a backwoods form of *bear.* Back when our country was young and sensible, anyone wishing to become a lawyer was first required to wrestle a fierce grizzly bear. In the unlikely event that the prospective lawyer won the match, he had "passed the bar" and was admitted to practice law (and was, incidentally, often subsequently sued by the bear for infliction of emotional damage). This was such a sensible system that as of 1846 there were only three lawyers in the entire United States, and they kept pretty much to themselves.

Oh, all right, that's not exactly true (although I'd like to point out that it's never too late to institute such a system). Your supposition, that the *bar* in question is the wooden one traditionally separating the lawyers, judge, and other interested parties from the riffraff in a courtroom, is correct. *Bar* has been used in the metaphorical sense since sixteenth-century England, when a lawyer admitted to practice before the court was said to have been *called to the bar*. This same *bar*, by the way, underlies the word *barrister*, which is what the British call lawyers who appear in court (as opposed to solicitors, who merely advise clients).

Incidentally, I believe your girlfriend may be a bit confused about what *raise the bar* means. The phrase actually comes from high jumping, where raising the bar makes things harder, not easier.

The BAR in question is the wooden one traditionally separating the lawyers, judge, and other interested parties from the riffraff in a courtroom.

Big Apple

Q: Why is New York City called the *Big Apple*?
—*Adele K., via the Internet.*

I'd call this question one of the hardy perennials of the word-origin biz, except that it's really more of a monthly. What's especially interesting is that a majority of folks asking about *Big Apple* do not live in New York City, which is virtually never referred to as the Big Apple by its residents. I guess this proves that advertising works. The term *Big Apple* was adopted in 1971 as the theme of an official advertising campaign aimed at luring tourists back to New York City. The ad campaign tried to recast New York, then generally perceived as noisy, dirty, and dangerous, in a more positive light by stressing the city's excitement and glamour.

Stablehands in New Orleans referred to New York racetracks as the BIG APPLE.

As to the origin of the term *Big Apple* itself, the prevailing wisdom for many years was that it was used in the 1930s, by jazz musicians in particular, but that no one knew where it first arose or how it became a synonym for New York City. Fortunately, Professor Gerald Cohen of the University of Missouri did some serious digging and uncovered use of the term *Big Apple* in the 1920s by a newspaper writer named John Fitzgerald, who wrote a horse-racing column (called "Around the Big Apple") for the *New York Morning Telegraph*. Fitzgerald's use of the term thus predated the jazzmen's *Big Apple* by about a decade.

It was still unclear where Fitzgerald got *Big Apple*, however, until Barry Popik, a remarkably persistent New York City slang historian, took up the search. Popik discovered that in 1924 Fitzgerald had written that he first heard the term from stablehands in New Orleans, who referred to New York racetracks as the Big Apple—the goal of every trainer and jockey in the horse-racing world.

Armed with the true story of *Big Apple* (and dogged determination), Popik spent the next four years trying to convince the New York City government to officially recognize Fitzgerald as the popularizer of *Big Apple*. In February 1997 he finally succeeded, and the corner of West 54th Street and Broadway, where John Fitzgerald lived for nearly thirty years, is now officially known as *Big Apple Corner*.

blackmail

Q: Please tell me what the origin of the word *blackmail* is. I have been told it has to do with freelance knights whose chain mail has turned black.

—*Norman L., Franklin Square, New York.*

I've never heard that theory, but it does make a certain amount of sense. So these unemployed knights, desperate for moola, became so unscrupulous that they started extorting money from people? And then their armor turned black, like a full-body mood ring? I like it. Among other things, it explains why so many lawyers wear dark gray suits.

Just kidding, of course. But the real story of *blackmail* is pretty interesting in its own right. In the first place, English now has two different *mails*, but it used to have three. The letter kind of *mail* is rooted in the old German word *malaha* or *malha*, meaning "pouch," which at first meant "any kind of pouch or bag" but was narrowed in the seventeenth century to mean "mail pouch." The "metal mesh armor" kind of *mail*, on the other hand, comes from the Latin *macula*, meaning "spot," referring to the holes in the mesh of chain mail armor.

Blackmail, meaning the extortion of money by the use of threats, especially threats to reveal secret or embarrassing information, comes from a third, now obsolete, sense of *mail*, meaning "payment" or "tax." This *mail* came originally from the Old Norse word *mal*, meaning "agreement," and exists as a word today only in Scots (the national language of Scotland) and some dialects in northern England.

Not surprisingly, the first blackmailers were corrupt politicians, Scottish chieftains who demanded protection money from local farmers. The farmers risked having their crops destroyed if they refused. The mail, or payment, was said to be black probably because the color black had long been associated with darkness and evil, but it might also have been because payment was usually made in livestock, rather than in silver, which was known as *white money*.

The "give me money or I'll burn down your farm" kind of *blackmail* first appeared in English around 1552, but by the early 1800s we were using *blackmail* to mean just about any sort of extortion, especially threatening to reveal secrets.

The first BLACKMAILERS were corrupt politicians.

EVAN MORRIS

blizzard

Q: Can you tell me where the word *blizzard* comes from? My English teacher thinks it might have been a German word.

—*Amy A., via the Internet.*

Funny you should ask. Actually, I must admit that I picked this question to answer because I am, as I write, firmly snowbound in a farmhouse in rural Ohio. At first the thought of not being able to go anywhere bothered me, but then I remembered that there's really nowhere to go out here anyway. So now I just sit by the window and watch the coyotes circling the house as darkness falls. I think they're after my grilled cheese sandwich.

This snowstorm isn't a true blizzard, the official criteria for which include sustained high winds and low visibility, but it certainly has given me the impetus to investigate the origins of *blizzard*. There seem to be a variety of theories about *blizzard*, many of which (the theories, not the storms) come from Iowa.

It turns out that Iowa more or less claims to have invented the word *blizzard*, a boast for which there is some evidence. The earliest known use of *blizzard* to describe a snowstorm was in the *Estherville (Iowa) Northern Vindicator* newspaper in April 1870. To hear the folks in Estherville tell it, a local character named Lightnin' Ellis coined the term, which rapidly spread around Iowa and then throughout the entire United States.

But (there's always a *but,* isn't there?) while the application of *blizzard* to a severe snowstorm may have been an Iowa invention, the word itself had already been around for quite a few years, meaning "a sharp blow or shot." Colonel Davy Crockett

used *blizzard* in the 1830s to mean both a blast from a shotgun and a verbal outburst, and the term was probably fairly well known even earlier. The use of *blizzard* to describe a violent storm was, it would seem, more of a logical extension than a true invention.

So where did *blizzard* come from in the first place? No one knows for sure, but it may well be onomatopoeic, designed to sound like the thing itself. After all, *blizzard* does sound like a blast of something, whether bullets, words, or blinding snow.

Iowa more or less claims to have invented the word BLIZZARD.

blockbuster

Q: My son (age six) and I were discussing where the word *blockbuster* came from because he and his mother were making a similar inquiry about *grapefruit* earlier in the day. I told him that I thought it was when the movie industry had a movie that was a smash, a great many people would gather at the movie houses and would crowd the sidewalks and maybe encompass an entire block around the theater. Would you please help us with this? —*Louis I., via the Internet.*

O.K., although I'm not entirely clear on the status of that *grapefruit* business. Did your son and his mother ever get an answer to their question? If not, tell them that grapefruit are called that because they grow in bunches, like grapes. If you or your son's mother went ahead and made up some other answer, you're on your own.

Your theory about *blockbuster* does make a certain amount of sense, since the term is almost always used today to describe a motion picture (or, less frequently, a novel or play) that becomes a "hot ticket." And movie fans certainly do line up around the block (or worse, camp out on the sidewalk for days) in search of tickets to such blockbusters.

The actual origin of *blockbuster,* however, is a bit grimmer than just another lame Hollywood schlock-fest. The term arose during World War II as Royal Air Force slang for an extremely large type of bomb, weighing as much as eight thousand pounds, so powerful that it was capable of destroying an entire city block. After the war ended, *blockbuster* was appropriated in the 1950s by the advertising industry, who added it to their arsenal of superlatives alongside *astounding, incredible,* and *revolutionary.*

The term arose during World War II as Royal Air Force slang for an extremely large type of bomb.

bloviate

Q: Help! For years I have been using the verb *bloviate* in reference to speaking in an overblown, self-important

If You Can't Say Something Nice, Say It Nicely.

As soon as human beings began to use language to communicate what they meant, they began to look for ways to disguise the meaning of what they said, or at least to soften the impact of their speech by avoiding words that a listener might find offensive or hurtful. *Euphemism* (from the Greek word meaning "to speak pleasantly") is the term for not saying what you mean, and over the centuries English has developed thousands of euphemisms, delicate stand-ins for direct and honest speech. Not surprisingly, euphemisms tend to be employed when the subject involves one of life's great anxieties: birth, death, sex, religion, wealth, poverty, and assorted bodily functions. Euphemisms also tend to reflect the public morals of particular times and places, and nothing sounds sillier to our modern ears than the taboos and euphemisms of a bygone age.

But the twentieth century will also be known for coining its share of ludicrous howlers that fool no one today and will supply the linguistic anthropologists of the future with hours of amusement. A brief sampling of the twentieth century's greatest weasel words and phrases.

associate: Low-paid clerk in a chain store such as Kmart or RadioShack.

away from his/her desk: Doesn't like you, won't talk to you, and wishes you'd go away. An important late-twentieth-century advance in telephone etiquette.

crowd management team: Riot squad.

culturally deprived: Raised in poverty, presumably without access to the opera.

efficiency: Tiny apartment without a real kitchen. A real-estate term justifiable only by the argument that it is "efficient" to be able to cook dinner without leaving the living room.

effluent: Toxic crud, most often industrial waste that has just been dumped into a previously clean river.

explicit: Pornographic.

frank exchange of views: Shouted threats.

loss prevention: Surveillance of customers (and often of "associates" as well, see above) in a store in order to prevent "inventory shrinkage" (theft).

no outlet: What replaced DEAD END on street signs.

poorly buffered precipitation: Acid rain. A term invented by the U.S. Environmental Protection Agency in 1982 to replace the dangerously clear term *acid rain* in official documents.

preowned: Used.

questionable: Blatantly illegal, immoral, and/or unethical.

sampling: Stealing the work (usually musical) of other artists, mangling it, and passing it off as your own.

travel center: Truck stop.

manner. Someone asked me about it the other day, and I went to the dictionary for a precise definition and *couldn't find it!* Panicked, I checked at least four other dictionaries (including two slang dictionaries, in case it was one of those humorous pseudoacademic words, like *absquatulate,* only based on *blow* instead of *squat*)—*no luck!* Is it true—does one of my favorite words not really exist? Have you ever heard or read it before? I couldn't have just imagined this, could I? I write from the precipice of madness. Pull me back.

—*J. M., via the Internet.*

Consider yourself pulled back from the precipice. You are not nuts—*bloviate* does indeed exist, and it means exactly what you thought it did. You've also discovered the same thing that I did when I went looking for *bloviate* late last year—most major dictionaries do not list the word. One that does is *Webster's Third New International Dictionary,* which defines *bloviate* as "to orate verbosely and windily," though I'm sure the term could be applied to writing as well.

You have even (and I hope you're not too disappointed) hit on the origin of *bloviate.* According to *Slang and Its Analogues,* a dictionary of British and American slang, published in seven volumes between 1890 and 1904, *bloviate* is (or was) American slang dating back to the mid–nineteenth century and probably arose as a fanciful variant of the slang term *to blow,* meaning "to boast."

One of the most famous practitioners of public bloviation was President Warren G. Harding, whose turgid prose prompted H. L. Mencken to note: "He writes the worst English that I have ever encountered. It reminds me of a string of wet sponges; it reminds me of tattered washing on the line; it reminds me of stale bean soup, of college yells, of dogs barking idiotically through endless nights. It is so bad that a sort of grandeur creeps into it. It drags itself out of the dark abysm . . . of pish, and crawls insanely up the topmost pinnacle of posh. It is rumble and bumble. It is flap and doodle. It is balder and dash." Now, *that's* bloviation!

bobby

Q: What is the origin of the word *bobby,* for a London policeman, and *beefeater,* for a Tower of London guard?

—*T. B., via the Internet.*

Nope. It's not going to work, pal. You're going to have to visit England for yourself, whether you want to or not, and you'll have plenty of opportunity to ask the bobbies and beefeaters in person when you get there. Why, just standing around waiting to see the changing of the guard at Buckingwhatsis Palace will provide you with twelve or thirteen hours to research all sorts of quaint English terms, not to mention lots of quaint

English people pressed right up against you who may actually know the answers. Later on, you can repair to the local pub and hoist a few pints with your new mates whilst (they talk like that over there) pondering the future of the country that invented a dish called *toad in the hole.* Have a nice time.

Oh, all right, I guess I'd better answer the question. *Bobby* as slang for any police officer (not just in London) is an allusion to Sir Robert Peel, home secretary in 1829, when the Metropolitan Police Act was passed, creating the modern English police force. Sir Robert also served as the inspiration for several other slang terms for coppers, among which were *peeler,* which is still heard in Ireland, and the now obsolete *Robert.* I guess "Cheese it, here come the Roberts!" just didn't cut it, slangwise.

Beefeaters are the guards at the Tower of London, known for their elaborate uniforms, which they have been wearing since the fifteenth century. I'm going to let you folks make up your own joke there. Anyway, opinions vary as to why they're called beefeaters, but the most likely explanation is quite literal. In the seventeenth century, *beef-eater* was a derogatory term for a servant who was well fed (by no means a certainty in those days), but a menial servant nonetheless. Nowadays, of course, even the lowliest wage slave can afford a Big Mac, so the term has lost its contemptuous sting, and beefeaters have become a treasured symbol of Britain's enduring grandeur. Incidentally, if you happen to actually meet a beefeater on your trip, please ask him what toad in the hole is.

Bob's your uncle

Q: I'm enclosing an article from *New York* magazine about a shop that recently opened in Manhattan called Bob's Your Uncle, the name of which is also evidently a common British expression. The writer of the article asked "ten different Brits" what the expression means and got ten different answers, ranging from "anything's possible" to "there you are." I'm hoping you can shed a little light on the question and, while you're at it, tell us who Bob is. —*Kathy M., New York.*

I'm looking at the clipping you sent along and coming to the conclusion that we have far bigger problems around here than figuring out who Bob might be. According to the author, Bob's Your Uncle (the store) specializes in "unlikely stuff put together in unusual ways"—specifically, "shirts on lamps, steel mesh on pillows, and pot scrubbers on picture frames." This sounds a great deal like the aftermath of some of the parties I threw in my youth. I never suspected there was a market for that mess. Does Martha Stewart know this is going on?

A popular sarcastic comment applied to any situation where the outcome was preordained by favoritism.

In any case, it is somewhat odd that "ten different Brits" didn't at least know what the phrase means, since *Bob's your uncle* is quintessential British slang, a way of saying "you're all set" or "you've got it made."

It all started back in 1887, when British prime minister Robert Cecil (also known as Lord Salisbury) decided to appoint Arthur Balfour to the prestigious and sensitive post of chief secretary for Ireland. Not lost on the British public was the fact that Lord Salisbury just happened to be better known to Arthur Balfour as *Uncle Bob*. In the resulting furor over what was seen as an act of blatant nepotism, *Bob's your uncle* became a popular sarcastic comment applied to any situation where the outcome was preordained by favoritism. As the scandal faded in public memory, the phrase lost its edge and became a synonym for "you're on easy street now."

booze

Q: Having been a bartender for quite a few years, I have often wondered about a word that has been tossed at me many times by both sober and not-so-sober individuals, namely *booze*. I would love to know where that word originated. I'm sure it would be an excellent "tip-getter."

—*Nicholas P., via the Internet.*

Before we begin, let me make sure I've got this straight. *I'm* supposed to research and explain the history of *booze*, whereupon people give *you* money. Doesn't seem quite fair, somehow. I'm gonna call my agent.

On the other hand, you're probably going to be earning those tips twice over just arguing against the erroneous stories your customers have heard about the origins of *booze*. One of the most persistent *booze* myths traces the word to the name of a distiller, often cited as *E. S.* (or *E. G.*) *Booz,* who produced whiskey in the Philadelphia area in the mid–nineteenth century. Evidently there was such a Mr. Booz, and he did market his booze in a distinctive bottle shaped like a log cabin, but his name is not the source of our *booze*.

For that, we must travel back five hundred years before the advent of Mr. Booz, to around 1300, when the Middle English word *bouse* appeared, meaning "to drink," especially to excess. We had borrowed *bouse* from the Dutch *busen,* meaning "to drink much alcohol," and we originally pronounced *bouse* to rhyme with *house*. But in the eighteenth century we started to pronounce it with a long "oo" sound, and our modern spelling of *booze* is actually a phonetic representation of that new pronunciation.

There was a Mr. Booz, and he did market his booze in a distinctive bottle, but his name is not the source of our BOOZE.

And as for our Mr. Booz of Philadelphia, while his name was not the source of the slang term, the coincidence that Mr. Booz sold a lot of booze probably did help popularize *booze* as a synonym for alcohol in the United States.

bosky

Q: In the Real Estate section of the *New York Times* recently, there was a reference to "Bucks County's bosky countryside." I remember my English teacher many years ago telling us that *bosky* meant "drunk" in Victorian England. Is this what the *Times* writer meant? Is there something going on in Pennsylvania we don't know about?

—*D. H., New York, New York.*

Only in Bucks County, which is the bit of Pennsylvania closest to New York City. Refugees from New York have overrun the place in recent years, and many of them, unable to accustom themselves to the nerve-racking absence of car alarms and random gunfire in their new abode, have retreated to the solace of the bottle. I myself spent two weeks in Bucks County on a recent Saturday afternoon, so I don't blame them a bit.

The slang sense of BOSKY was based on likening drunkenness to being lost in the woods.

Just kidding, of course. I think, to get back to your question, that the *Times* writer must have been hitting the old thesaurus pretty hard when he or she wrote that article. The primary meaning of *bosky* is "bushy" or "wooded"—the Middle English word *bosk* came from the same root that gave us *bush.* The writer simply meant that Bucks County has a lot of trees and bushes compared to, say, Times Square.

But *bosky* did, as you recall, also mean "drunk" in eighteenth- and nineteenth-century English slang. J. S. Farmer and W. E. Henley, in their classic *Slang and Its Analogues,* defined *boskiness* as "the quality of being fuddled with drink." Their theory was that the slang sense of *bosky* was based on likening drunkenness to being lost in the woods. Perhaps, but I think Farmer and Henley missed the point. All those trees, all those bushes, all those cows just standing there looking at you—that's what drives a city dweller to drink in the first place.

brand-new

Q : I have always been puzzled by the phrase *brand-new*. Recently I was reading a magazine or newspaper and saw this phrase spelled *bran-new*. Can you tell me which is correct and what the origin of this odd phrase is?

—*Mary Schmidt, Chicago, Illinois.*

Well, I was all set to tell you that the *bran-new* that you saw must have been a typographical error, but when I checked the *Oxford English Dictionary*, *bran-new* was listed as an accepted alternate form of *brand-new*. I still believe, however, that what you saw was a typo, based on the almost universal use of *brand-new*.

I'll bet that it's the *brand* in *brand-new* that is really the source of the mystery of the phrase for you. After all, the things that we buy are rarely branded in the cowpoke sense of the term, unless we collect cows. And while most goods we buy are of a particular brand, that doesn't seem relevant to the item's newness, as anyone who has ever bought a used Ford can attest.

The answer to our little mystery lies in the original meaning of the noun *brand*, which was "a burning or fire," in this case specifically a furnace, forge, or kiln. Something brand-new was an item, whether pottery or forged metal, fresh from the

Something BRAND-NEW was an item, whether pottery or forged metal, fresh from the fires of its creation.

fires of its creation, and the phrase dates back to the late sixteenth century. Shakespeare used the expression "fire new" to mean the same thing.

The "brand-name" sense of *brand*, incidentally, is from a somewhat different sense of *brand*—this time as a verb, meaning "to mark with an iron hot from the fire." The first brands in this sense were probably wooden casks of wine marked in this fashion with the vintner's trademark. The term for the practice of branding cows and horses with a rancher's brand comes from the same source.

brass tacks

Q: I was in a trivial debate with a friend when he decided it was time to "get down to brass tax," which made me chuckle. I replied that he was free to do what he liked, but I preferred to get down to "brass tacks." He replied that that made no sense, and I replied, "Well, like brass tax makes a whole lot of sense." Anyway, I know I am right, but I cannot figure out what the origin of this phrase is.

—*David O., via the Internet.*

I'm going to play psychic for a moment here and guess that this exchange with your friend took place in print, probably through e-mail, since *brass tax* certainly sounds just like *brass tacks* when spoken aloud. Am I right or am I right? Eat your heart out, Kreskin.

You are indeed correct about the proper phrase being *get down to brass tacks,* meaning "to seriously concentrate on basic facts," but beyond that I'm afraid my crystal ball gets a little murky. We do know that *brass tacks* first appeared in the late nineteenth century, but there are a number of theories as to where it came from and what role, if any, real brass tacks played in its origin.

Probably the most popular theory about *brass tacks* traces the phrase back to old general stores, where fabric was sold by the yard. It is said that brass tacks were driven into the counters of such stores exactly one yard apart to aid in measuring the fabric, supposedly leading to the saying "Don't guess; get down to brass tacks."

Rhyming slang substitutes one or two rhyming words for the concealed "real" word.

Another theory traces the phrase to the brass tacks used in nineteenth-century furniture manufacture. In this scenario, *get down to brass tacks* would mean to judge the basic soundness of a chair, for instance, rather than its upholstery.

While neither of those theories is implausible, I, in my psychic wisdom, lean toward a third explanation. *Brass tacks,* many authorities believe, began as Cockney rhyming slang for "facts." Rhyming slang, which sprang from the nineteenth-century London underworld, substitutes one or two rhyming words for the concealed "real" word (*trouble and strife* for "wife" being the standard example). The advantage of this theory is that it would mean that *brass tacks* has always had its current meaning of "basic facts."

break a leg

Q: I do quite a bit of work in our community theater and have been exposed to most of the theater lingo. However, last night, a fellow volunteer and I were wondering about the origin of the phrase *break a leg*. I always thought it had something to do with dancers, but she said she had heard the phrase dated back to early theater, where there were actually wooden structures on the front of the stage called *legs*. If the show went well and was well received, an audience member would celebrate by seizing one of these legs and breaking it. I have never heard of this, and it sounds a bit illogical to me. Who is right (if either of us is)?

— Sarah P., via the Internet.

Oh, it doesn't seem so illogical to me. When I enjoy a theatrical performance, I always make a point of destroying part of the stage on my way out of the theater. If I really like what I've seen, I sometimes even wait around outside and beat up the actors.

Speaking of legs, are you certain yours isn't being pulled? Your friend's story is by far the most bizarre explanation of *break a leg* I've ever heard, and that's saying something.

"Break a leg," of course, is how actors wish each other good luck before a performance, and has been commonly heard in the theater since the early twentieth century. That date of origin, by the way, casts serious doubt on one of the more colorful theories about the origins of the phrase. It has been said that *break a leg* is a reference to the assassination of President Abraham Lincoln in Ford's Theatre in Washington, D.C., by the actor John Wilkes Booth in 1865. In attempting to flee the scene, Booth jumped from Lincoln's box to the stage, breaking his leg. The fact that actors didn't start wishing each other good luck by saying "Break a leg" until more than fifty years after Lincoln's assassination makes this an unlikely source.

All of which puts us back at square one, but fortunately the late Eric Partridge rides to our rescue. Partridge is to the collection and documentation of slang what Shakespeare is to the theater, and in his *Dictionary of Catch Phrases* he has quite a bit to say about *break a leg*. After dismissing the John Wilkes Booth story, Partridge explains that he favors the theory that *break a leg* originated as a translation of a similar German catchphrase, *Hals- und Bienbruch,* with which German actors wish their colleagues "a broken neck and a broken leg." The German phrase seems to have begun life among aviators, possibly during World War I, and gradually spread to the German theater and then to the British and American stages.

But why, I hear you ask, would someone wish injury and ill fortune on a comrade embarking on a perilous mission? Simple: popular folklore down through the ages is full of warnings against wishing your friends good luck. To do so is to tempt evil

Popular folklore down through the ages is full of warnings against wishing your friends good luck.

spirits or demons to do your friend harm. Better to outwit the demons (who must be rather dim, it seems to me) by wishing your friend bad fortune

The charm doesn't always work, of course. The stage directions for opening night of the reconstructed Globe Theatre in London a few years ago called for two actors to swing dramatically from a balcony down to the stage on ropes. One of the actors slipped and, you guessed it, broke his leg.

bupkes

Q: The word *butkis* came up in my ESL class today, and I didn't know the origin. I was thinking that it is a portmanteau word, but I hope the roots aren't that crude.

—*Nathan C., Celaya, Mexico.*

Don't worry; they're not. But first we have to back up a bit and explain to the folks out there in readerland just what a portmanteau word is. *Portmanteau* is a very old and fancy word for what we today call a suitcase. Originally it meant an officer who carries (French *porte*) a prince's mantle *(manteau),* or ceremonial robe, but later came to be applied to any sort of valise or traveling bag.

The term *portmanteau word* was invented by Lewis Carroll (pen name of Charles Dodgson) in his *Through the Looking Glass* to mean "a word that combines both the sound and the meaning of two other words." Thus *slithy,* as Carroll explained in "Jabberwocky," meant both "lithe" and "slimy." One of our classic modern portmanteau words is *motel,* which combines *motor* and *hotel.* The matter of just what words might be combined to produce the object of your inquiry is, I think, best left as an exercise for the reader.

Meanwhile, back at *butkis,* there's a small problem that renders most of the above discussion moot (although still, I hope, enlightening). The word you're looking for is not *butkis.* It's *bupkes* (also spelled *bubkis, bupkis,* and *bubkes*), which is Yiddish for "beans," or, figuratively, "nothing, nada, zilch." But there's more to *bupkes* than just "nothing." When you say you got bupkes from a deal you brokered, for instance, it really means you got nothing when you should have gotten at least something if there were any justice at all in this world. All of which is a lot for one word to say, but Yiddish is good at that.

Bupkes can also mean "an offer so low as to be an insult." As the late Leo Rosten noted in his 1968 classic, *The Joys of Yiddish, bupkes* is a howl of outrage often heard in the cutthroat world of show business: "Four weeks he worked on that sketch, and what did they offer him? Bupkes with bupkes!"

There's more to BUPKES than just "nothing."

Burton, gone for a

Q : An English friend recently replied to an e-mail I'd sent her three months ago, excusing the delay by explaining that in the interim her computer had "gone for a Burton." Whatever *gone for a Burton* means, it must have happened again, because I can't get her to explain who the mysterious Burton is. Any ideas? —*A. K., via the Internet.*

Gone for a Burton is a British slang term that translates roughly as "out to lunch," "missing," or, applied to a machine such as your friend's computer, "not functioning."

It seems to be generally accepted that *gone for a Burton* is World War II–vintage Royal Air Force slang, having first appeared in print in 1941. The original meaning of the term was a bit of black humor, much grimmer than the modern usage. It referred to a flier (at best) missing or (at worst) killed in action, someone who had, in the equivalent American phrase of the same period, "bought the farm."

The question of who or what the Burton in question might have been, however, has led to several theories. Montague Burton, goes one explanation, was a firm of tailors in Britain known for its fine suits. According to this theory, the phrase sardonically suggested that a missing flier had gone off to be fitted for a suit.

The most convincing explanation, however, traces *Burton* to prewar British advertising. The popular line of Bass ales were brewed in the town of Burton upon Trent in Staffordshire, England, and a glass of ale was known colloquially as simply a *Burton.* Ev-

It referred to someone who had, in the equivalent American phrase of the same period, "bought the farm."

idently the Bass brewery sponsored a series of advertisements shortly before the war, each of which involved a situation in which one person was clearly missing, as indicated by an empty chair at a dinner table or the like. The tag line of each ad was the same: "Gone for a Burton."

Since this phrase was already imprinted on the public imagination by the advertisements, it would have been a logical candidate for a catchphrase used to explain the disappearance of a comrade in battle.

busboy

Q: Could you tell me the origin of the word *busboy*? Who started using it? — *G., via the Internet.*

Someone who wasn't a busboy, that's for sure. I've always found the term a bit demeaning, myself, although "busboy" is one of the few job descriptions I haven't filled at one time or another. I did work as a waiter in an all-night coffee shop for a few days in the late 1960s. The proximate cause (as lawyers like to say) of my sudden departure from waiterland was a tableful of hippies with a raging case of what used to be called the *munchies*. They ordered nearly everything on the menu, ate it all, and then attempted to pay their tab with good vibes. My boss decided that I should foot the bill, I demurred, and that was that.

Having done a bit of research on *busboy,* however, I think that this somewhat belittling name for a restaurant worker who sets and clears tables might be repaired by returning it to its original form. Busboys were known in the late nineteenth century as *omnibuses,* a term that came from the Latin *omnibus,* meaning "for all." *Omnibus* was a popular word in the nineteenth century, with a variety of uses, having first been applied to the large public horse-drawn coaches that marked the first appearance of urban mass transit. The motorized descendants of these omnibuses are known today, of course, as *buses.*

While busboys of the period may or may not have ridden to work on buses, they were known as *omnibus boys* or *omnibuses* themselves because their job was to do anything and everything that might be useful in the restaurant. *Omnibus* in this restaurant sense first appeared in 1888, and the first written example of the shortened form *bus-boy* has been traced to a 1913 issue of the *Industrial Worker* (the newspaper of the Industrial Workers of the World, or Wobblies, by the way), although the word was almost certainly in use long before then.

BUSBOYS were known in the late nineteenth century as *omnibuses.*

butterfly

Q: What about *butterfly?* My *American Heritage Dictionary* opines that the word comes from the thought that they steal milk and butter. A more colorful thought is that the word is an alteration of *flutter-by* (if any animal can be thought to flutter, it would be a butterfly). A second thought is less poetic: that butterflies are flylike animals that favor the pistils and stamens of flowers, the part of the flower that is sometimes the yellow color of butter. Any thoughts?

— *Scott S., via the Internet.*

Oh boy, a bug question. I love bugs. Yessiree, love those bugs. Actually, I hate bugs, and unfortunately my New York City apartment building has a problem with humongous water bugs every summer, which wreaks havoc with both my nerves and my writing. These brazen bugs waltz boldly into my study and march right toward me in broad daylight, leaving me, as defender of my hearth and home, no choice but to stand on my desk until they leave. Then I go to the movies for a day or two in case they come back.

There was a theory in the Middle Ages that the little critters stole milk and butter.

Butterflies, I know, are supposed to be beautiful and all that, but to me they're still bugs. I suspect that the fluttering business is just a ruse to lull us into complacency, whereupon they'll zoom down and . . . well, never mind. Anyway, no one knows where butterflies got their name, although the theory endorsed by your dictionary does have some evidence to back it up. Apparently the German word for butterfly is *milchdieb,* which translates as "milk thief." Evidently there was a theory in the Middle Ages that the little critters stole milk and butter, a myth possibly inspired by their light, colorful wings, which in many cases could be said to resemble milk or butter. Or perhaps they really did steal milk and butter. It's not impossible.

Tee Many Martoonies

When early man discovered the dramatic effects of alcohol on the human noggin, people at once began dreaming up terms for drink, drinkers, and drunkenness. So profound has the influence of alcohol on human society been, in fact, that some of the oldest words in English are drinking terms. And once we invent a good drinking metaphor, we often use it for hundreds of years. *To wet one's whistle*, for instance, has meant "to take a drink" since Chaucer's time, more than five hundred years ago, yet it can still be heard in any corner pub today.

Herewith a small sampling of some other colorful terms in our collective Drinkers' Dictionary.

bend the elbow: To take a drink, since the eighteenth century, later shortened to *bender*, meaning a "prolonged bout of drinking."

bootleg: Unlicensed booze peddlers in the nineteenth century often concealed pints of moonshine in the tops of their high boots, thus earning themselves the name *bootleggers*. It is not known where they hid the beer nuts. In any case, bootlegging hit the big time when Prohibition outlawed liquor in 1920, and large-scale bootlegging operations spawned fortunes for entrepreneurs from Al Capone to Joseph Kennedy. By the time happy juice was legal again, *bootleg* had become a handy term for anything sold illegally.

drunk: Perhaps the best measure of the eternal popularity of drinking is the astounding number of slang synonyms for *drunk* that have appeared over the last few hundred years. Apart from the obvious *stewed, juiced, crocked* (from the crocks used to store liquor), *buzzed, loaded,* and the like, some of the more unusual terms invented to describe inebriation include *embalmed, crooked, fishy, fried, full of* courage, *soused, fur-brained, having a brass eye, hearing the hoot owl, having a shine on, having a guest in the attic, carrying a turkey on his back, shellacked, pot-shot, below the mahogany* (i.e., lying on the floor under the bar), *having a brick in the hat, polluted, bulletproofed,* and *hicciusdoccius* (from the hiccups sometimes induced by drinking).

groggy: If a night of pub-crawling leaves you feeling dizzy, sleepy, and groggy, cheer up. That's not just an alcoholic buzz you've got there—it's an honored naval tradition. Sailors in the seventeenth-century British navy looked forward to their daily ration of rum as one of the few bright spots in an otherwise fairly grim existence aboard ship. But in 1740, Admiral Edward Vernon decided that his sailors would perform more efficiently if he diluted their rum with water. Vernon was already known as Old Grog among his men because of the grogram (a coarse wool fabric, from the French *gros grain,* "large grain") coat he wore. So Old Grog's new recipe was immediately dubbed *grog* by his understandably cranky sailors, a term that spread when the Royal Navy as a whole adopted the weakened mixture as standard shipboard fare. Today we use *groggy* to mean "fumbling" or "fuzzy-headed," even when not due to alcohol.

teetotaler: One who rigorously abstains from drinking any alcohol. There is general agreement that the first use of *teetotal* in reference to alcohol was in a speech to an English temperance society by a man named Richard Turner in 1833. While some of his contemporaries drew a moral distinction between beer and hard liquor, Turner urged his listeners to abstain from all alcohol. Contrary to popular legend, there is no evidence that Turner recommended tea as an alternative to alcohol, or that his listeners were urged to mark the letter *T* for *total abstinence* on their pledge cards at the meeting. The *tee* tacked onto the front of *total* was just a common way of giving extra emphasis to a word at that time, and you could just as well be teetotally broke or teetotally tired as teetotally sober.

Another theory is that butterflies got their name because (I kid you not) their excrement is said to resemble butter. I think we can safely say that whoever thought this one up was pretty clearly spending too much time around butterflies and/or buying very low grade butter.

cabal

Q: I read somewhere, but I don't remember where, that *cabal* is an acronym derived from the names of five men. The last name, I believe, was Lauderdale. Could you enlighten me on the other four names (if this is really the origin of the word)? —*Mark S., via the Internet.*

Well, yes, I could tell you the other names, but then, according to rules laid down by the Language Columnists Cabal, you'd have to take over writing this column for the next ten years, and I'm not sure you're ready for that.

Cabal is actually one of my favorite words. It means, of course, "a small group of people engaged in secret intrigues, especially of a sinister nature." The key word here is *sinister,* and the great thing about *cabal* is that the word itself even sounds sinister. A cabal is not simply a clique or club. A cabal has a purpose and a plan, both invariably nefarious. Cabals manipulate global currency rates. Cabals do not hold bake sales.

The theory you've heard about *cabal* sounds like the one that traces the word back to the government of King Charles II of England in the late seventeenth century. Five of the king's ministers happened to have names (Clifford, Arlington, Buckingham, Ashley, and Lauderdale) the initials of which, purely coincidentally, spelled out *cabal*. The king's political opponents made much of this spurious acronym at the time, but their accusations of secret plots among the king's ministers only made sense because *cabal* was already being used to mean "a small circle of conspirators."

The actual origin of *cabal* is much older. It comes from the Hebrew *qabbalah,* meaning "tradition," the name given to a mystical interpretation of the Old Testament developed by medieval rabbis in the thirteenth century. By the middle of the seventeenth century, both *cabbala* and *cabal* were being used in a secular sense to mean "secret" or "mystery" or "a small group of conspirators who kept mysterious secrets."

CABALS manipulate global currency rates. Cabals do not hold bake sales.

Catch-22

Q: What is a Catch-22, and what is the term's origin? I've heard the term used many times but still cannot gather what it means even by looking at what the words around it are. — *Cassandra J., via the Internet.*

Go ahead, make me feel old. Next you'll be asking me what *crash pad* means. Actually, I knew I was hopelessly over

Joseph Heller
had really only
given a name to
a particularly
modern sort of
bureaucratic
conundrum.

the hill a few years ago when an inquisitive twenty-something asked me, in dewy-eyed innocence, "Were the Beatles at Woodstock?" Oh yes, absolutely, of course. And so were Benny Goodman, John Philip Sousa, and that Brahms dude.

I am supposing that your not knowing what *Catch-22* means is evidence of your relative youth because the phrase is of fairly recent vintage and made quite a splash when it arrived in popular usage. *Catch-22* is the title of a novel published in 1961, written by Joseph Heller and based on his experiences as a World War II bomber pilot in Europe. The central character in *Catch-22* (which you really ought to read, by the way) is the bombardier Yossarian, whose all-too-accurate perception of the futility and insanity of war leads him to seek a psychiatric exemption from flying further combat missions. But Yossarian runs smack into what Heller dubbed Catch-22 (*catch* in this sense meaning "snag"). As Heller put it, "There was only one catch and that was Catch-22. . . . If he flew them [more missions] he was crazy and didn't have to; but if he didn't want to he was sane and had to."

In inventing *Catch-22,* Joseph Heller had really only given a name to a particularly modern sort of bureaucratic conundrum, a bit of circular logic in which one thing is dependent upon another, which is in turn dependent upon the first thing. More mundane examples of Catch-22s would be needing a driver's license to get to Motor Vehicles to take your driving test or, my personal favorite, needing to be rich to effectively avoid paying income tax.

caught red-handed

Q : My daughter asked me where the phrase *caught red-handed* came from. I have heard different stories, ranging from the red dye "bombs" that banks put in the bags of money that robbers run off with, to an older version that involves pistachio nuts and workers eating the profits and getting caught with their hands stained. If you can help me with this, I'd appreciate it very much. — *Ryan M., via the Internet.*

Well, it is my sad duty to tell you that both stories you have heard about *red-handed* are wrong. But I really like the one about pistachio pilferers. It reminds me (oh no, here he goes again) of my brief but brilliant career as night manager of an all-night carryout in a large, unnamed Midwestern city. Maybe they've gotten around to naming it by now. Anyway, we had one of those nut cases (we actually had a lot of nut cases, but I digress) full of peanuts and pistachio nuts and, my personal favorite, cashews. I could (and did) eat cashews for hours on end. Then one night the boss came in and said, "Gosh, we've sold a lot of cashews this week," and suddenly I knew it was time to go be a newspaper columnist. Life gives you those signals sometimes.

The history of the fifteenth century may clue you in to what the "RED" really was: blood.

The phrase *red-handed,* meaning "in the act of committing a crime, exhibiting incontrovertible evidence of guilt," is quite a bit older than exploding bags of money or even organized nut theft. It first appeared in that form in English in the mid–nineteenth century and was common as the adjective *redhand* in Scots even earlier, in the fifteenth century. A moment's consideration of the history of the fifteenth century may clue you in to what the "red" really was: blood. A murderer caught red-handed still had the blood of his victim on his hands. We have, since the eighteenth century, used *red-handed* to describe any criminal caught in the act or bearing irrefutable evidence of guilt.

cheesy

Q: My friends and I are curious as to the use of the word *cheesy* to mean something chintzy or somehow inferior. When did this start? What is the reference? While we are on the subject, we are also wondering about the word *corny*.

— *Cathy F., via the Internet.*

It does seem odd that we use *cheesy* to mean "tasteless," "cheap," or "shoddy." After all, from Velveeta to brie, cheese is one of everyone's favorite foods. I may be overstating that a bit, but I do happen to own a twenty-year-old cat who, frail as she is, will still make your life miserable should you forget her daily slice of cheese. In any case, this negative sense of *cheesy* has been around since about 1863 and is thought to have arisen as an allusion to the unpleasant smell of overripe cheese.

Speaking of cheese, one of my favorite cheese metaphors from my years as an office worker turns out probably to have nothing to do with cheese. Being the naturally insubordinate type myself (hard to believe, I know, but true), I often referred to whatever supervisor held sway over me at the moment as *the big cheese*. I have since discovered that the *cheese* in question does not, as I had imagined, mean "a wheel of cheese" but is thought to be a mutation of the Urdu (a form of Hindustani) word *chiz,* which simply means "thing." Phrases such as *the real chiz* were popularized by nineteenth-century Anglo-Indian hipsters in Britain, but since *chiz* didn't ring any bells for most English speakers, it was eventually anglicized to *cheese.*

As for *corny,* meaning "trite," "overly sentimental," or "schmaltzy," we can probably trace the term to, believe it or not, the mail-order seed catalogs popular in turn-of-the-century America. To hold their customers' interest, seed firms would sprinkle jokes, cartoons, stories, and riddles throughout their catalogs. The jokes, being of singularly low quality, came to be known as *corn catalog jokes,* which was then shortened to simply *corny* and eventually applied to anything considered embarrassingly unsophisticated.

This negative sense of CHEESY is thought to have arisen as an allusion to the unpleasant smell of overripe cheese.

chortle

Q: In today's edition of the *Dallas Morning News,* Jim Wright used an excellent word that I have not seen "in a coon's age," that being *chortle.* I believe this means to chuckle or laugh, but I am not sure. Nor am I sure of the source of the word. Can you help?

—*John W., Allen, Texas.*

Chortle is indeed an excellent word, and your guess about its meaning to chuckle or laugh is absolutely correct. *Chortle* more specifically means "to chuckle or laugh in a cheerful, kindly, and joyful way," and I think that "cheerful and kindly" shade of meaning may be why we don't see *chortle* very often these days. Thanks to our increasingly gossip-obsessed

 This is the era of the smug sneer, the sly snicker, and the derisive laugh. A kindly CHORTLE doesn't stand a chance.

culture, this is the era of the smug sneer, the sly snicker, and the derisive laugh. A kindly *chortle* doesn't stand a chance.

That's a shame, because *chortle* is a remarkable word, among the very few successful English words that are known to have been coined by a specific person. The inventor of *chortle* was none other than Lewis Carroll (real name Charles Dodgson), the author of *Through the Looking Glass* and *Alice's Adventures in Wonderland.* Not surprisingly, given his fantastic imagination, Carroll was fond of inventing his own words. *Chortle* made its debut in his *Through the Looking Glass* in 1872, in "Jabberwocky," the extraordinary poem-within-a-fable that begins,

> 'Twas brillig, and the slithy toves
>   Did gyre and gimble in the wabe;
> All mimsy were the borogoves,
>   And the mome raths outgrabe.

At the end of the poem, after the fearsome Jabberwock has been slain, Carroll writes,

> "And has thou slain the Jabberwock?
>   Come to my arms, my beamish boy!
> O frabjous day! Callooh! Callay!"
>   He chortled in his joy.

It was never entirely clear what Carroll meant by *chortle* (though some authorities think the word is a combination of *chuckle* and *snort*), but that didn't stop people in the late nineteenth century from adopting the word. And we (some of us, anyway) have been chortling ever since.

chum

Q: I found an interesting word in a *New York Times* article recently about how skippers of boats off the California coast take tourists out to see sharks and encourage the latter to congregate by luring them with buckets of blood, fish parts, and a pig's head or two thrown in the water. This practice is referred to as *chumming*. I wonder what the derivation is— perhaps it's as simple as it sounds. Naturally, the surfers don't appreciate it, but as one said, "You don't have to outswim the sharks, just your buddy!" *— George B., via the Internet.*

I missed that particular article in the *Times,* but judging from what you've said, tourists in California must be pretty hard up for excitement. The average shark is dumb as a box of rocks and about as much fun to watch. Whatever happened to going to Disneyland? Then again, maybe the real fun comes from watching the sharks chase the surfers—that sounds like a typically Californian pastime.

It occurs to me that I'm not entirely certain what you mean by "perhaps it's as simple as it sounds." Tossing a pig's head or two in the water would indeed strike many sharks as a friendly ("chummy") gesture, but knowing how most fishermen regard sharks, that origin of the term seems unlikely. That "friend" sense of *chum,* by the way, dates back to seventeenth-century England and is generally thought to be a student slang contraction of *chamber-mate,* or "roommate."

CHUM SALMON takes its name from a Chinook word meaning "spotted or striped."

As to the "throw fish guts in the water in order to attract sharks" sense of *chum,* all the dictionaries I've consulted maintain a discreet "origin unknown," noting only that the word is of American origin and first appeared in the mid–nineteenth century.

But I have a suspicion that *chum* in this sense may be related to a fish common to the Pacific known as the *chum salmon,* which takes its name from a Chinook word meaning "spotted or striped." Perhaps this chum salmon was so frequently chopped up and used as chum that its proper name became a generic term for "chopped-up fish." But as I said, it's only a theory, so I'll just throw it in the water and see what it attracts.

church key

Q: The term *church key* is used to describe a bottle opener. What is the derivation of this term?

—*Uncductape, via the Internet.*

This is one of those queries I receive about twice a month, a frequency that raises a question that has been percolating in the back of my own mind for a while. Does anyone actually use church keys anymore? I'm not much of a drinker, but I was under the impression that twist-off caps had become the rule. But maybe that's just on the high-class wines we get out here in Ohio.

The classic church key was a handy little gizmo and usually combined a can-top piercer (a nasty pointy thing used in the days before pop-tops) on one end with a bottle-top prier-offer on the other. They were usually made of heavy steel and often emblazoned with the engraved logo of a local gas station. I'm sure someone out there is collecting these things.

They were usually made of heavy steel and often emblazoned with the engraved logo of a local gas station.

In any case, the relevant fact about these bottle openers is that some of them did indeed resemble large, old-fashioned keys, possibly to the sort of large, old-fashioned doors often found on churches.

As to why these little gadgets came to be known as *church keys* in particular, the answer is simple: irreverence. It might be a bit hard to believe in this age of *America's Sleaziest Home Videos,* but when *church key* first appeared as slang for a bottle opener in the early 1950s, it was considered a mildly shocking and even borderline sacrilegious term. Using the phrase *church key* in refined company in those days would have produced the same mixture of raised eyebrows and guilty chuckles as referring to the rump of a roast turkey as the *pope's nose* (as my father delighted in doing).

clean your clock

Q : What is the origin of the phrase *clean your clock* (as in beat up)?　　　　　　　*—Jean B., via the Internet.*

Golly, can't we all just get along? When I was a young'un and my friends and I were mad at someone, we'd just order fifteen pizzas to be delivered to his house. Of course, we also knew that the local pizza was so vile that one bite of those pies would render digestive vengeance of biblical proportions on our foe, so maybe a punch in the schnoz isn't so bad in comparison.

To begin at the beginning, *clock* has been slang for the human face since the mid–nineteenth century, based on the supposed resemblance of a clock face to the human face. (We're talking analog clocks here, obviously. If anyone in your family resembles a digital clock, call NASA immediately.) *Clock* as a verb has also been slang for "to punch in the face or strike violently" since the early twentieth century, again based on the clock-face metaphor.

Elsewhere in the world of fisticuffs, *clean* has been slang for "vanquish" since the early nineteenth century. *Fix someone's clock* has been a slang term for "to finish someone" since about 1908, first attributed to the writer O. Henry. Curiously, the first written example of the entire phrase *clean someone's clock* that anyone has yet found dates only back to 1959, but we can assume it had been around for a while before that.

Even with all this evidence tying faces and punches together, I must say that there is another possible source for *clean someone's clock*. In railroad slang, an engineer who applies the train's air brakes in an emergency is said *to clean the clock* or *wipe the gauge* as the speedometer needle drops to zero. It seems logical that such a graphic metaphor would be the perfect way to describe stopping an opponent in his tracks.

CLOCK has been slang for the human face since the mid-nineteenth century, based on the supposed resemblance of a clock face to the human face.

cobweb

Q: I'm curious about the origin of the word *cobweb*.

—*Steve W., via the Internet.*

Funny you should ask. Cobwebs are, of course, the network of fine filaments spun by a spider as a trap for its prey, and thereby dangles a major beef of mine. As I may have mentioned before, Word Detective World Headquarters maintains a branch office in rural Ohio. WDWH-OH occupies a stately old Victorian farmhouse with many charms, the most dubious of which, however, is the fact that it apparently does double duty as the community center for Spidertown, USA. I had no idea that there were so many varieties of spiders on this planet, or that so many of them were so large as those that greet me in the shower every morning. And I have discovered that there's nothing so bracing on a cool, dark autumn evening as walking out your front door into a cobweb so huge that its owner must eat whole chickens for lunch. It's gotten to the point that even an old copy of *Charlotte's Web* gives me the whim-whams.

There's nothing so bracing on a cool, dark autumn evening as walking out your front door into a COBWEB so huge that its owner must eat whole chickens for lunch.

So anyway, we all know what a web is (aside from being the most pointless part of the Internet), but here's an interesting tidbit for dictionary fans. The root of *web* was a prehistoric Germanic word that also gave us *weave*. The Old English word for "one who weaves" was *webster,* which is now obsolete as a noun but still exists, of course, as a proper name.

But the real question is where the word *cob* comes in. The most commonly encountered *cob* is in *corncob,* the cylindrical woody shoot on which grains of corn grow. That kind of *cob* comes from a very old English word that meant "head" or "top."

It is possible that *cobweb* is related to that word, but a more certain ancestor is the Middle English *coppe,* which meant simply "spider." Over the years *coppe* was gradually slurred to *cob,* and, voilà, *cobweb.* But now I must take my leave. Both of my cats are staring with a disturbing intensity at the ceiling directly above my head.

coleslaw

Q: Would you kindly advise the etymology of *coleslaw?*

—*Della S., via the Internet.*

I don't know if this is true in the rest of the United States, but if you go into a coffee shop or diner in New York City and order nearly anything on the menu, you'll find that your meal comes with a small paper tub of coleslaw perched on the edge of the plate. The remarkable thing is that no matter where you dine, the coleslaw always looks and tastes exactly the same. Now, I'm not exactly Sherlock Holmes, but one day recently the truth finally dawned on me. Somewhere out there is a huge factory, a humongous Central Coleslaw, concocting this stuff by the ton, loading it onto huge trucks, and shipping it to diners all over the city in the dead of night.

Coleslaw, of course, is a salad made from shredded or chopped cabbage. What else goes into coleslaw depends on which dictionary you read. The *Oxford English Dictionary*

No matter where you dine, the COLESLAW always looks and tastes exactly the same.

prefers the cabbage "dressed with salt, pepper, vinegar, etc., eaten either raw or slightly cooked," while the *American Heritage Dictionary* states tersely, "dressed with mayonnaise." Both recipes omit mustard, a serious oversight in my opinion, but then again, it's probably not a good idea to use dictionaries as cookbooks in the first place.

Coleslaw takes its name from the Dutch *koolsla,* which is a shortened form of *koolsalade,* itself drawn from *kool* (cabbage) plus *salade* (salad, pronounced "sla"). Children, many of whom have not studied Dutch, often refer to coleslaw as *cold slaw,* a mutation that makes so much sense that it is listed as an alternate form in many dictionaries. *Coleslaw* first showed up in English around 1794.

We coleslaw fans know that it is probably one of the healthiest things to eat in a diner. What we really want to know is, who puts it in those little tubs?

come a cropper

Q: For years I have seriously wondered about the origin of the phrase *to come a cropper.* I have tried to look it up in all the places it should have been, but to no particular avail. Do you know? I have suspected that it may have origins having to do with foxhunting or with horses hurdling, or trying to hurdle, over various unnatural obstacles. Any knowledge about this that you can pass on to me would be very much appreciated.   *—Sherrie B., via the Internet.*

Aha! Here we have, at last, proof positive of what I've been trying to tell newspaper editors for years. The average reader doesn't give a dingo's yelp about the deficit or global warming or the Spice Ladies and all that trendy folderol. No, your average reader is still trying to figure out some arcane idiom you invoked in one of your "think pieces" years ago. "H. R. Haldeman's attempts to shield President Nixon may come a cropper"—ring a bell? It should. It's been driving poor Ms. B. around the bend for more than twenty years.

Thank heavens she appears to be mildly psychic. *To come a cropper* does indeed come from the world of horse riding and racing. The original phrase was *neck and crop,* describing a fall from a horse where the rider is thrown headlong over the horse's head. The most common occasion for this sort of extremely unpleasant accident is when the horse stops short of a jump, as in a steeplechase, but the rider keeps going. *Neck and crop* itself refers to the horse's head, *crop* being another word for "throat."

As a metaphor for failure, *come a cropper* graduated from the world of equestrian mishaps to general use in the mid–nineteenth century. Anthony Trollope illustrated the new sense perfectly in his 1875 novel *The Way We Live Now:* "He would be 'coming a cropper rather' were he to marry Melmotte's daughter for her money, and then find that she had got none."

> The average reader doesn't give a dingo's yelp about the deficit or global warming or the Spice Ladies and all that trendy folderol.

---

continuously/continually

Q : Did I fall asleep for a few years or something? It seems that *continually* has replaced *continuously* to describe something that happens constantly or without interruption. I know they are synonyms, but is there a reason for the switch? Seeing *continually* used everywhere continuously bugs me!

—Pete B., via the Internet.

Yeah, Pete, you were out like a light. You missed everything. We tried to wake you when they repealed the subjunctive mood, and again when they legalized dangling participles (the TV newscasters had been lobbying hard for that one), but no dice. Not a peep from you.

So the English language is a complete shambles, but at least someone around here is well rested. And now that certain someone is upset because they messed with his adverbs while he was snoozing. Well, tough, buddy, you'll just have to muddle through with the rest of us. That's officially spelled *thru* now, by the way.

I have no idea why people have started to use *continually* instead of *continuously,* but then I never understood the macarena, either. Some things just happen. There is indeed a commonly accepted tradition that *continuously* is used to describe a process or action that proceeds uninterruptedly ("The car alarm wailed continuously from 3 A.M. to dawn"). *Continually,* however, is usually used to describe an action that may come and go but is

EVAN MORRIS

We tried to wake you when they legalized dangling participles (the TV newscasters had been lobbying hard for that one), but no dice.

habitual or routine ("The car alarms continually blaring made the neighborhood a poor choice for poets").

But while this usage is traditionally observed, there is nothing in the history or structure of either word that would make the rule compelling. *Continually,* in fact, was around and serving both uses for more than 350 years before *continuously* even showed up.

So, is there a difference? Yes, in recent tradition at least. Does it matter which you use? Not a whole lot, especially since no one is paying attention. I happen to like the distinction between *continuously* and *continually,* but I'm fully aware that I'm out of the loop on this one. I also like big band music and cloth napkins. No wonder I never understood the macarena.

copper-fastened

Q: The *Irish Times* has been doing a fair bit of political reporting about the E.U. lately, and they seem to use the phrase *copper-fastened* quite frequently to indicate when something is finis; signed, sealed, and delivered; done. Where does it come from? Does it have anything to do with Mr. Levi Strauss? Or roofs? Barrels? Policemen?

— *Stephen R., Dublin, Ireland.*

Avast Ye Lubbers . . .

Sailing the sea is one of humankind's oldest endeavors, so it's not surprising that the lingo of both ancient and modern mariners has been rich and varied. What is remarkable is that so many nautical terms with technical meanings that are barely (if at all) comprehensible to the average landlubber (a sailor's term of contempt, from *lubber,* meaning "stupid fellow") have been adopted as standard English idioms here on terra firma. Here are a few such everyday terms and phrases still carrying a whiff of the open sea.

fish or cut bait: Make up your mind; quit dithering. The allusion is not, as is commonly thought, to a dawdling angler being urged to cut his or her fishing line (that would be a waste of line, hook, and bait). *To cut bait* means to prepare bait (usually "junk" fish) for use as either hooked bait or "chum" dumped into the water to attract other fish. There are really only two jobs on a fishing boat: fishing, and cutting the bait. The phrase really means, "Pick what you're going to do, and do it."

groundswell: In metaphorical use, a slowly increasing level of support for, or opposition to, a politician or policy (as in "Recent polls reveal a groundswell of support for legislation that would outlaw many of journalism's most cherished clichés"). A real groundswell is a deep swell or motion of the sea, usually produced by storms far out in the ocean.

leeway: The amount of variation, or "play," allowable in any situation. The lee (from the Old English *hleo,* "shelter") side of anything is the side away from the wind. *Leeway* in the original nautical sense (1669) is the amount that a ship may be blown sideways off course by the wind and sea. (It's the angle between the ship's heading and its actual course, if you want to get technical.) A competent skipper will always be certain that enough leeway is allowed in the ship's course to avoid drifting aground.

maelstrom: Tumult, uproar, confused ruckus. The original Maelstrom (from the Dutch *malen,* "to grind or whirl around," and *stroom,* "stream") was (and is) a huge whirlpool off the west coast of Norway, held responsible for the loss of many ships.

maroon: To strand; to place someone in a position from which they cannot escape. *Maroon* comes from the Spanish word *cimarrón,* meaning "wild" or "untamed." Maroons were originally runaway slaves in the West Indies who, having escaped their bondage, fled into the forests and mountains of the islands to live. The nefarious practice of seventeenth-century pirates and buccaneers of abandoning their captives on deserted islands also became known as *marooning. Marooned* eventually came to mean simply "lost in the wilds."

swashbuckler: A swaggering braggart, adventurer, or ruffian; originally a derogatory term, lately adopted by investment bankers to affectionately describe the most rapacious of their breed. Created from the antiquated words *swash* (to make a noise by striking) and *buckler* (shield) around 1560, *swashbuckler* originally meant a mediocre swordsman who compensated by making a great deal of noise, strutting through the streets banging his sword on his shield. Although the real swashbucklers were mostly cheap bullies, swashbuckling got a romantic spin in dozens of Hollywood swashbucklers—pirate movies made in the 1940s starring the likes of Douglas Fairbanks Jr. and Errol Flynn.

turn a blind eye to: To deliberately ignore or overlook, especially to ignore a breach of regulations or decorum. In 1801 Lord Horatio Nelson, later architect of the final British victory over France at Trafalgar, was second in command of a British fleet besieging Copenhagen. Nelson believed that the time was right to attack, but a junior officer pointed out that the fleet commander had sent up flags ordering his forces to withdraw. Nelson, who had lost an eye in a previous battle, put that blind eye to his spyglass, announced that he didn't see any such signal, and ordered the ships in his squadron to attack. Fortunately for Nelson, his attack succeeded, so his superiors turned a blind eye to his blatant insubordination.

Oh goody, another opportunity to demonstrate my abysmal ignorance of global political developments. I do know that *E.U.* stands for *European Union,* a splendid scheme that requires all you Yurpeens to drink Belgian wine, use unisex bathrooms, and translate all your street signs into French, right? I may have a few of those details a bit wrong, since the average American (a species of which I am a pretty fair specimen) reacts to TV news reports about the European Union by exclaiming "Eeeyooo!" and changing the channel.

Fortunately, I just happen to have a roomful of reference books, which gives me a leg up on finding the answer to *copper-fastened.* Apparently, the term arose in reference to sailing ships. Since copper bolts resist corrosion by salt water and sea air, a ship constructed employing such materials was considered especially well made and durable. The first use in print of *copper-fastened* anyone has come across dates back to 1796. The figurative use of *copper-fastened* to mean, as the *Irish Times* uses it, "a done deal" or "a sure thing" would certainly seem to be a logical extension of the term. Here in the United States, where the Wild West is a more common source of metaphors than is the graceful age of sail, we use the term *bulletproof* to mean roughly the same thing.

The term arose in reference to sailing ships.

cul-de-sac

Q : Isn't the word *cul-de-sac* a French word? Well, what the heck does it mean? We just bought a house on a "cul-de-sac." —*J. B., via the Internet.*

Oops. Um, wouldn't it have been a good idea to pin down the meaning of *cul-de-sac* before plunking down your hard-earned moola for an abode resting on one? Well, it's water under the bridge, so to speak, I suppose.

Yes, *cul-de-sac* is indeed a French word. One of the most terrifying of all French words, in fact.

Ready? *Cul-de-sac* translates into English as "huge radioactive swamp full of giant mutant frogs." Bummer, eh? On the bright side, I'm sure the nice mortgage folks will still be writing to you when your happy home is nothing more than a residual green glow hanging in the miasmic swamp air.

Hey, old pal, are you still with us? I was just kidding. No real-estate agent would dream of selling you a home on top of a huge radioactive swamp. Next door to one, maybe, if the schools were good.

Cul-de-sac actually translates as "bottom of the bag" and means any sort of vessel or thing that is closed at one end, like a bag. In the case of a street, a cul-de-sac is one that has no outlet except the entrance and is also known as a *dead-end street.*

Given the doggedly upbeat bent of most real-estate agents, it's not surprising that they shy away from such terms as *dead-end,* with all its negative connotations, in favor of a classy-sounding

French term like *cul-de-sac.* And that literal translation, *bottom of the bag,* sounds way too much like *bottom of the barrel* to be useful.

I actually spent many of my formative years living on a cul-de-sac in suburban Connecticut, and I can testify that there was one major advantage to the arrangement. Angelo, the local Good Humor ice cream man, had to pass my house both coming and going on his daily route, giving me plenty of time to extort dimes from my mother. Yes, back and forth Angelo drove, all summer long. Until the giant mutant frogs got him, of course.

Real-estate agents shy away from such terms as *dead-end,* in favor of a classy-sounding French term like CUL-DE-SAC.

cup of joe

Q: I have been trying to find the origin of the term *joe* in reference to coffee. *A cup of joe* sounds American and/or military in origin, but I can't seem to find anything definitive. Any help you could provide would be appreciated.

—*Michael C., via the Internet.*

Call me a hopeless romantic who watches too many old movies, but I've always wanted to duck out of a torrential downpour into a small diner in a bad part of town, hoist myself up on a stool, slap a quarter on the counter, and growl, "Cuppa Joe, Louie, and make it strong and black." I'm planning to actually try this someday, as soon as I find a trench coat that fits. I just hope Louie doesn't ask me, "Regular or decaf?" That would ruin the whole thing.

Meanwhile, back at your question, there is, alas, no definitive answer to the riddle of *joe* as slang for "coffee." *Joe* in this sense first appeared around 1930. It may be a variant of *java,* also a popular term for coffee since the nineteenth century, when the island of Java, in Indonesia, was a major source of the world's coffee.

> I've always wanted to duck out of a torrential downpour into a small diner in a bad part of town, hoist myself up on a stool, slap a quarter on the counter, and growl, "CUPPA JOE, Louie, and make it strong and black."

Another theory, and one that rings true to me, is that *joe* as slang for coffee might be derived from *joe* as a synonym for "the common man," as in "a regular joe." This use of *joe* as a generic name for the man in the street dates back to around 1911 and was very widespread in the military services, as in *G.I. Joe,* which was slang for the common soldier long before it became the name of a toy. Since *joe* as slang for coffee was and is especially common in the U.S. Navy, and since the navy pretty much runs on coffee, it seems logical that the military slang term for an average guy could have been extended to the average guy's usual beverage.

One thing's for sure, though. These days, Louie's going to want more than a quarter for that "cuppa joe."

decimate

Q: Please help my colleagues and me. We wonder whether the word *decimate* originated in relation to the behavior of the Roman Empire, the Nazis, or some alternative source. —*Befuddled, via the Internet.*

Befuddled, eh? I think I went to high school with your sister, Bewildered.

In regard to your multiple-choice question, we can safely pin *decimate* on the Roman Empire, specifically the Roman army. Faced with a mutiny by their troops (which, given conditions in the Roman army, was probably not an infrequent phenomenon), the Roman commanders would sometimes order one out of every ten soldiers to be executed as an example to his comrades. *Decimate* itself comes from the Latin word *decimare,* meaning "to take or destroy one-tenth," which came in turn from *decem,* the Latin word for "ten."

Words change their meanings over time because they are, first and foremost, tools of human communication.

Another concurrent meaning of *decimate* was "to exact a tax of one-tenth," but it's the grisly "kill every tenth person" meaning that has survived to the present day, and thereby hangs a tale of disputed English usage. Starting in the middle of the seventeenth century, many people started using *decimate* in a looser sense to mean "destroy or kill the greater part of" something. Since *decimate* in its strict "one-in-ten" sense has become (thank heavens) less applicable in the modern world, most people have had no objection to the slight change in meaning.

Occasionally, however, you will hear some self-appointed guardians of the English language rail loudly about the "real" meaning of *decimate* and bemoan its modern "misuse" as a symptom of linguistic degeneration. Ignore them. Words change their meanings over time because they are, first and foremost, tools of human communication. And anyone who objects to the modern use of *decimate* to mean "kill or destroy most of something" should feel free to write me. On parchment, with a quill pen. And have it delivered by a carrier pigeon, of course.

dog is hung, until the last

Q: I've been looking for the origin of the phrase *till the last dog is hung* without success. I believe its meaning is similar to *till the cows come home* but find it hard to believe that anyone ever actually engaged in hanging canines either before or after the cattle were brought in for the night. Perhaps the dogs in question were of the human persuasion. Any ideas? — *Gil O., via the Internet.*

Well, at the risk of seeming misanthropic (which, of course, I am), I must say that I certainly hope that such a ghastly phrase doesn't refer to actual dogs. I've come to the conclusion lately that the admirable qualities so often sought among human beings actually reside almost exclusively in dogs. I think that the least we should do is allow Fido and Sparky to vote in our elections. It certainly can't hurt.

I myself first heard this phrase about ten years ago, used in the sense of "sticking it out until the bitter end," making it somewhat different from *till the cows come home,* which usually means either "very late at night" or "never." Most of the examples of *until the last dog is hung* I have found use it in reference to bar patrons hanging around until closing time or guests reluctant to leave a party until forced to do so.

There is, fortunately, some reason to believe that, as you suggest, the dogs in question were human. Some sources trace the phrase to the use of *dog* since the fourteenth century to mean "despicable person" and theorize that *until the last dog is hung* may have come from the informal system of criminal justice practiced in the American West in the eighteenth and nineteenth centuries. Since the first citation for the phrase in print dates back to 1863, this certainly seems possible. It's easy to picture a cowboy doggedly vowing to pursue a band of outlaws "until the last dog is hung," that is, until the last criminal is brought to justice. It's also easy to imagine that line being a pivotal moment in a movie western or two, which may have helped keep the phrase alive over the years.

> The admirable qualities so often sought among human beings actually reside almost exclusively in dogs.

dogsbody

Q : I've heard the expression *dogsbody,* I believe in reference to a servant. Where did it come from?

—*Norm H., via the Internet.*

No wonder it's so hard to get good help these days. If I referred to my manservant Dustly as my *dogsbody,* my wardrobe would be a dog's breakfast in a flash. You didn't know columnists had manservants, did you? Of course we do. It's in our standard contract, same clause as the polo ponies and the silk dressing gowns. Why do you think Bill Gates writes a newspaper column? For the money? Well, yes, but it's also the only way he can get a decent manservant.

There was always a need for good words to describe those lower on the food chain than oneself, preferably nice, disgusting epithets.

Actually, a dogsbody is both more and less than a simple servant. Primarily a British phrase, *dogsbody* means "a subordinate or drudge who handles a variety of menial tasks," or what we Americans would call a *gofer* (one who "goes for" things).

As to the origin of *dogsbody,* we can thank that peerless font of wisdom, culture, and culinary refinement, the British Royal Navy. Seamen in the eighteenth century were evidently often served something referred to as *pease pudding,* made by boiling dried peas and/or sea biscuits in a cloth. It sounds disgusting, it undoubtedly was disgusting, and the sailors, no fools, didn't call the ghastly mush *pease pudding.* They called it *dogsbody,* an affectionate term probably based on its taste, texture, and hypothetical pedigree.

Since no navy, least of all the Royal Navy, is a democracy, there was always a need for good words to describe those lower on the food chain than oneself, preferably nice, disgusting epithets. *Dogsbody* certainly fit the bill, and beginning in the early twentieth century the word came to be used to mean "any junior officer or midshipman expected to run errands or perform menial chores for his superiors." As use of the term gradually broadened beyond naval use, it became less pejorative and more a simple synonym for "assistant" or "menial worker."

doughboy

Q: A social studies teacher I know is trying to find out why American infantrymen in World War I came to be known as *doughboys.* My dictionary also refers to the term *doughfoot* as having the same meaning. Did it have something to do with feet that were swollen like rising dough?

—*Jan L., via the Internet.*

The human mind is a funny thing, especially, apparently, mine. I read your letter and, being a good American consumer, immediately thought of cute little Poppin' Fresh (or however you spell his infernal name), the Pillsbury Doughboy of a thousand TV commercials. Sad, isn't it? You probably won't be surprised to learn that I used to own a cat named after a popular fabric softener.

There turns out to be quite a bit of controversy about the

origin of *doughboy* as a slang term for a soldier or infantryman, but one certainty is that the term is much older than most people would suspect. Although it gained currency in popular use during World War I, *doughboy* first showed up in print in 1847, before the American Civil War. General George Armstrong Custer's widow mentioned the term in her memoirs, written in 1887, explaining that doughboys were doughnuts often served to sailors aboard ship. According to Mrs. Custer, the term was applied to infantrymen because the large brass buttons on their uniforms reminded someone of these naval doughboys. Lending support to at least the culinary aspect of Mrs. Custer's theory is the fact that *doughboy* has meant "a boiled flour dumpling" to sailors since about 1685.

General George Armstrong Custer's widow mentioned the term in her memoirs, written in 1887.

There are other theories about *doughboy,* such as those tracing the term to the adobe clay barracks that housed soldiers in the American Southwest at that time *(adobe boys* becoming *doughboys),* or to soldiers using adobe dust to whiten their white uniform belts, or to soldiers' boots' being caked with adobe mud. None of these theories is impossible, but neither is any especially convincing.

If I had to pick a theory, I'd say that it's most likely that doughboys owed their moniker to those little doughnuts Mrs. Custer mentioned—not because the soldiers wore buttons that resembled them, but because doughboys were a staple of the military diet at the time, and a slang term for sailors and soldiers, perhaps *doughboy-eater,* gradually became simply *doughboy.*

And the cat was named Snuggles, by the way.

doughnut

Q: It is mindless to defend *donut*. It is better to admit *doughnut*, as a nut made of dough. But I suspect the origin is *dough-naught*. Naught, after all, is round like a donut. And like a zero. They could have been called *dough-zeroes*. April is the crullers month.

—*Richard A., Little Rock, Arkansas.*

Now hold it right there, bucko. It may be mindless to defend *donut*, a spelling that rivals *quik* and *thru* for annoying stupidity, but actual doughnuts could use some defending at the moment. Under attack by the Health Police merely because each tender morsel harbors enough saturated fat to stun a yak, doughnuts may soon fall victim to the same puritanical dietary jihad that robbed us of bacon and Twinkies. Well, they'll get my doughnuts when they pry them from my cold, powdered-sugar-flecked hands.

The problem with your theory about doughnuts getting their name because they resemble zeroes is twofold. First, the earliest recorded use of *doughnut*, in Washington Irving's account of life in 1809 New York, makes it clear that he is refer-

Not only are Krispy Kreme DOUGHNUTS to die for, but they spell the word *doughnut*, not *donut*.

ring to "dough nuts"—"balls of sweetened dough, fried in hog fat." The Dutch who settled New York called them *oliekoeks,* a name still in use in Irving's day. Second, these primordial doughnuts had no holes—and where there is no hole, there is no zero. Today, of course, most doughnuts have holes, and doughnuts in their original form (little balls fried in fat) are sold as *doughnut holes.* Go figure.

Speaking of the defense of doughnuts, I am doing my part by wearing, at every opportunity, a snazzy baseball cap that I bought at a Krispy Kreme doughnut shop last year. Not only are Krispy Kreme doughnuts to die for, but they spell the word *doughnut,* not *donut.*

draconian

Q: Where was Draconia, that place where that authoritarian came from?   —*Ian D., via the Internet.*

Ah, yes—hail, Draconia, Land of Enforcement. How we miss her dank dungeons, her kangaroo courts, her dainty thumbscrews, and her sturdy truncheons. And they didn't put up with any of that wimpy due process hoopla in Draconia, bucko, though you were always welcome to consult your lawyer. You could usually find him in the cell next door.

Just kidding, sort of. There never was a specific place called Draconia, though a good argument could be made that there's a little bit of Draconia in every human society. As an adjective, *draconian* means "excessively rigorous, harsh, and cruel" and is

Draco is said to have declared, "Small crimes deserve death, and for great crimes I know of no penalty severer."

almost always used in reference to a regime or set of laws or punishments. Naturally, one society's or historical period's "draconian punishment" is often another's "simple justice," and your cultural mileage may vary. Blinding or maiming a person convicted of theft, for example, is considered a draconian punishment in most, but not all, parts of the world. Capital punishment, current public enthusiasm notwithstanding, is considered draconian in most advanced nations except the United States and Japan.

While there never was a Draconia, there was most certainly a Draco, and that's where we got the adjective *draconian*. Draco, whose name, appropriately, means "dragon" in Greek, was a lawmaker in ancient Athens in a time of popular unrest. The Athenians were at the point of revolt over unequal treatment under the then-current system of laws, so Draco instituted a new set of laws guaranteed to shut folks up. Under the new Draconic code of 621 B.C., almost everything, from murder to cursing in public, was punishable by death. Questioned about the wisdom of such a one-size-fits-all approach to justice, Draco is said to have declared, "Small crimes deserve death, and for great crimes I know of no penalty severer."

Unfortunately, the term *draconian* was not retired with Draco's laws and has gone on to enjoy an uninterrupted applicability to instances of cruel "justice" throughout human history up to today. One does not ordinarily wish that words would become obsolete, but in the case of *draconian*, I think most people would make an exception.

EVAN MORRIS

dud

Q: I come from England, and fifty-five years ago I worked in the accounting office of a large department store. In those days (as now) people bought on time, popularly known as the *never-never,* as most people didn't pay off their accounts for years. When we determined they might not pay, we put *DD* (for *doubtful debt*) after their name. When we determined they would never pay, we put *DUD* after their name, for *doubtful unrecoverable debt.* I was told that this is where the word *dud* comes from. Is this true?

— Stanley L., West Long Branch, New Jersey.

Oh, so I'm a "dud" now, am I? What ever happened to all that "valued customer" folderol you department-store feather merchants used to heap on me? Ah, but that was before the weatherproof boots you sold me dissolved at the first hint of rain, wasn't it? Before the toaster explosion? And before the deranged riding mower you sold me attacked the deputy sheriff called to subdue the homicidal washing machine I bought . . . guess where? Excuse me, pal, but I've already paid in spades.

Meanwhile, back at your question, I'm afraid that the story you were told is not the origin of *dud,* a word that has been around since the fifteenth century. Although the ultimate origins of *dud* are shrouded in mystery (that sounds a lot better than "we don't know," doesn't it?), its original meaning was "an article of clothing," a sense we still use in the term *duds*. (That same sense of *dud* gave us the word *dude*, by the way.)

Dud eventually came to mean "tattered clothes," and by the seventeenth century, scarecrows, attired in cast-off clothing, were being called *dudmen*. Sometime in the nineteenth century we began to use *dud* to mean "anything counterfeit, ineffective, or fraudulent," a usage that got a big boost during World War I, when unexploded artillery shells were called *duds*. Today, almost anything that fails to live up to our expectations, be it a Hollywood blockbuster that fizzles or a blind date who drools, can be labeled a *dud*.

eighty-six

Q: O.K., I've got a term I already know the meaning of but am still unsure about the origin of—the term *eighty-six*. I know that it means two things (mostly dealing with bars and restaurants): "out of something in the kitchen" ("We're eighty-six on lettuce!"), and "to be kicked out for being disorderly or drunk." I understood from a few years ago that the origin of the phrase is back in Old New York (in the early twentieth century). When they started just building bars and houses and apartments pretty much alike, the city code guys would figure all bars were the same and therefore set the same maximum occupancy

EVAN MORRIS

at, you guessed it, eighty-five. Therefore, Mr. Eighty-six was, well, "eighty-sixed." If you have any other possible clues on this, I would be appreciative. I know you're the Word Detective, but why not numbers, too? —*Alan W., via the Internet.*

Why not numbers, indeed? Except, of course, that I have a long-standing pathological fear of numbers. That's why I have so much trouble turning in my income tax forms—I can't even stand to look at them, much less mail them. I'll get to your question in a moment, by the way. I'm busy establishing an alibi here.

The theory you've heard about *eighty-six* is certainly entertaining but almost certainly untrue. Among other problems with it is the fact that many of the large drinking houses on the Bowery in the nineteenth century routinely accommodated far more than eighty-five patrons, and I think that "maximum occupancy regulation" business is of fairly recent vintage anyway.

Bars do loom large in EIGHTY-SIX lore.

But bars do loom large in *eighty-six* lore. Another popular theory traces *eighty-six* to the street address of Chumley's, a venerable New York saloon. Unruly Chumley's patrons forcibly ejected into the street, the story goes, would often find themselves recumbent on the sidewalk, gazing up at the number 86 on the door. Unfortunately, there's not much evidence supporting that theory, either.

What we do know is that *eighty-six* first appeared as "kitchen slang" meaning "out of that item" in the 1930s and fairly quickly came to mean "stop serving that customer" as well. Eventually, *eighty-six* spread to general usage, where it came to mean simply "dismiss" or "quash" ("The boss eighty-sixed my proposal for beer in the lunchroom").

Probably the theory with the most logic behind it is that *eighty-six* began as rhyming slang code of the sort found in London's Cockney underworld of the nineteenth century. As *trouble and strife* meant "wife" in rhyming slang, so *eighty-six* may have stood for "nix," meaning "nothing" or "to dismiss." How *eighty-six* then ended up in U.S. restaurants is a bit of a puzzle, but I'm afraid it's the best theory anyone has come up with so far.

Esq.

Q: I work at a professional placement firm, and my curiosity is piqued by the usage of *Esq.* after certain individuals' names on some résumés. This has nothing to do with an earned degree, does it? The dictionary I consulted described *esquire* in terms of knightly rank, and then as "a title of courtesy." Are these people (usually attorneys) just trying to sound more accomplished? —*C. S., via the Internet.*

The short answer to your question is yes, and I think that if you go back and check, you'll find that all those "Esq.-ies" hold law degrees. The use of *Esq.* has become completely identified with the legal profession.

EVAN MORRIS

The rationale for lawyers adopting *Esq.* is that it provides the same professional identification for them as *M.D.* does for doctors and *Ph.D.* does for academics. As for *Esq.* being pretentious, I would agree, and a quick check of the origin of *esquire* illustrates that the practice is also just plain silly. The word itself comes originally from the Latin *scutum,* or "shield," and an esquire was originally a young manservant (a squire) whose job consisted of holding a knight's shield and similar lowly tasks. With the passing of knights, *esquire* came to be applied to any young man of "noble" birth who lacked a title such as *prince* or *duke.* Eventually the term was broadened to include just about any young man. I remember receiving mail addressed to me as *Esq.* when I was about fourteen years old, so I've never been able to regard the lawyerly *Esq.* with anything approaching the awe intended by those who affect the title.

Part of the appeal of *Esq.* for lawyers is said to be that the title has become genderless and thus can be used by female as well as male lawyers, although the formerly popular tag *attorney-at-law* certainly doesn't address the sex of the addressee. A more likely reason for the popularity of *Esq.* is that it is thought to bestow an aura of exalted social rank on the wearer.

As for ESQ. being pretentious, I would agree, and a quick check of the origin of *esquire* illustrates that the practice is also just plain silly.

Sounds Like . . .

The simplest way to invent a word for a particular thing or action is simply to imitate the sound the thing or action itself makes.

If early man, for example, did not have a word for the act of belching, but he wanted to make fun of one of his cave mates' eructations after a large meal of roast mastodon, he might simply have imitated the sound by pointing to the belcher and exclaiming, "Gurk! Gurk!" Assuming his friends did not respond by clobbering him with a rock, he would have invented a successful new word meaning "to belch": *gurk.*

As a matter of fact, *gurk* is a real English word that does mean "to belch," and it did arise as an imitation of the sound of a belch. Etymologists call words formed by imitating the sound (or sometimes the feel) of an action or thing an *echoic* (since it echoes the sound) or *imitative* formation. (If they're feeling fancy, they call it an *onomatopoeic* creation, from the Greek for "making words.")

English is full of words that are either wholly or partly echoic, which makes English speakers either very economical or very lazy, depending on your perspective. Some obviously echoic words, such as *bang, boom, pop,* and *slam,* crop up in our conversation almost every day, but here are a few of the less obvious ones.

chuckle: Formed on the verb *to chuck,* meaning "to make a sound like a chicken," *chuckle* originally meant "to laugh convulsively" back in 1598. But by 1803 *chuckle* had settled down and meant "to suppress a laugh," probably to avoid offending the chickens. *Giggle* is also echoic, as is *guffaw.*

cough: Pretty obvious once you think about it. *Cough* first appeared in English in the fourteenth century, but its linguistic ancestors go back to prehistoric times.

cricket: From that incessant *creek-eet*ing. Also since the fourteenth century.

fanfare: A short, flourishing tune, probably originally a trumpet call to hunting hounds, now often played to alert press photographers when someone important enters the room. Appeared in the eighteenth century, presumably in imitation of the sound of horns.

fuss: "A needless or excessive display of concern about anything" *(OED)* since about 1700, *fuss* probably arose in imitation of something or someone sputtering, huffing, and puffing as if highly excited.

gush: From the Middle English *gosshe,* the sound of rushing water.

helter-skelter: Pre–Charles Manson, it meant "in a confused, disorganized, and hasty manner"; it is thought to be echoic of the sound of many feet rushing around.

jerk: Originally (around 1550) a lash with a whip, later generalized to mean a sudden pull (as in "a jerk on the reins"), the word *jerk* itself ends suddenly, as if with a jerk. The meaning "stupid person" is recent (around 1935) and probably originally referred to someone from a "jerkwater" town, a remote backwoods stop lacking a water tower, requiring train crews to "jerk" water from nearby streams to fill their boilers.

Ping-Pong: A simple imitation (from around 1900) of the sound of the ball being hit back and forth by two players. Still a trademarked term in the United States, by the way.

pump: A very old word occurring in various forms in several European languages, *pump* first appeared in English around 1440 and probably echoes the sound of water being pumped.

throb: Whether it's your heart or your headache, *throb* has been imitating that violent beating motion since around 1362.

eureka

Q: Please help me find the origin of the word *eureka*. Was it credited to Alexander Graham Bell, or is there some connection with Nebraska.   —*H., via the Internet.*

Nope. There is not, to my knowledge, any connection between *eureka* and either Alexander Graham Bell or Nebraska. *Eureka,* of course, is primarily used as a joyous interjection, the sort of thing you shout out when you're excited and very happy. Mr. Bell did invent the telephone, an accomplishment that might (opinions vary) have merited a whoop of "Eureka!" but there is apparently no evidence that Bell whooped any such thing. As for Nebraska, I'm sure it's a very nice state, but it probably doesn't rate a "Eureka!" either, and if you're thinking of the city called Eureka, that's in Kansas. (There's one in California, too. In fact, "Eureka" is the state motto of California.)

Archimedes jumped out of the bathtub and began racing through the streets of Syracuse stark naked, shouting, "EUREKA! EUREKA!"

The origin of *eureka* lies in ancient Greece, where, according to legend, a certain King Hiero II of Syracuse commissioned a goldsmith to fashion a new crown for him. The king suspected that the artisan had shorted him on the gold content of the crown by substituting a cheaper metal, silver, and turned to the philosopher Archimedes for a way to prove his case. Archimedes then did what any philosopher faced with a real-world problem would do: he went and sat in his bathtub. While getting into the bath,

EVAN MORRIS

however, Archimedes realized that the water rose as he sat down. He also realized that gold, being denser than silver, would displace less water than silver, and that the honesty of the king's goldsmith could be measured by just such a simple test. When Archimedes realized all this, goes the story, he jumped out of the bathtub and began racing through the streets of Syracuse stark naked, shouting, "Eureka! Eureka!" which is Greek for "I have found it!"

What Archimedes had discovered, of course, is the modern method of measuring the specific gravity of an irregular solid by immersing it in a bathtub with an old Greek philosopher. The goldsmith did turn out to be cheating, by the way, and probably ended up wishing he'd stayed in his own bathtub that morning.

exception proves the rule

Q: I'm having a colloquy with a copy editor colleague here at *PC World* magazine. Does *the exception that proves the rule* in fact mean the exception that disproves the rule? Or that by some circumlocution the exception in fact serves to prove the rule correct?

—*Barbara L., via the Internet.*

If we ever held a contest to pick the most frequently misunderstood popular saying in English, *the exception that proves the rule* would be a hands-down winner. It seems as though an exception to a rule would prove only that there are gaping holes in the rule and that it might not be much of a rule to begin with, right?

Well, in the first place, the phrase was originally "The exception proves the rule," leaving out the *that*, which doesn't add anything and can only cause more confusion.

To properly understand "The exception proves the rule," we need to take a look at the very old legal maxim from which it came: "Exception proves (or confirms) the rule in the cases not excepted" ("Exceptio probat regulam in casibus non exceptis," for you Latin fans). In the original legal sense, this described situations in which an authority granted an exception to a rule in a special case but, in making such an exception, confirmed that in general the rule was valid and should govern in all other cases. After all, if the rule weren't fundamentally valid, the judge wouldn't be making an exception to it—he or she would be throwing out the entire rule. It's analogous to a parent letting a child stay up late on New Year's Eve. Such bending of the rules on a special occasion doesn't mean bedtime has been abolished from then on.

"Exceptio probat regulam in casibus non exceptis," for you Latin fans.

It's important to note that "The exception proves the rule" doesn't work very well when applied to the natural sciences, which are ruled by physical laws, not judges or parents. In the fields of physics or chemistry, for example, an unexpected result of an experiment must necessarily call into question (and possibly disprove) your whole hypothesis. The universe is not a lenient parent and does not make exceptions to its laws.

factoid

Q: What can you tell me about *factoid?* I was watching CNN last week with my father-in-law when one of those little factoid boxes (where they tell you some interesting tidbit of news, such as how many hamburgers were sold last year at the Moscow branch of McDonald's) came on the screen. My father-in-law snorted and said that if CNN knew what *factoid* really meant, they'd never use the word. So I'm confused— what does *factoid* really mean?

—*Dan G., Brooklyn, New York.*

Your father-in-law is a wise man. Heed his words. If he snorts, it means that you should be snorting, too. If he offers you a job, take it. He is, among other things, evidently one of the few people left who remember what *factoid* originally meant.

Factoid is one of those rare words that were undeniably invented by an identifiable individual, in this case Norman Mailer, in his book *Marilyn,* published in 1973. The *Oxford Dictionary of New Words* defines *factoid* thus: "A spurious or questionable fact; especially something that is supposed to be true because it has been reported (and often repeated) in the media, but is actually based on speculation or even fabrication." Norman Mailer himself defined *factoids* as "facts which have no existence before appearing in a magazine or newspaper, creations which are not so much lies as a product to manipulate emotion in the Silent Majority."

Mailer invented the word by combining *fact* with *oid,* a scientific suffix meaning "resembling or having the form of, but not identical to." Something that looks like a fact but isn't, in other words. Needless to say, factoids in Mailer's sense are the antithesis of serious reporting, and to accuse a journalist of trafficking in factoids was a grave insult, at least until CNN came along.

Mailer's original negative definition of *factoid* was a valuable contribution to the language on a par with George Orwell's *Newspeak,* and, in this age of spin doctors and tabloid journalism, *factoid* still fills a conspicuous need. Perhaps we should petition CNN to give us our word back.

To accuse a journalist of trafficking in FACTOIDS was a grave insult.

friend in need

Q: Does "A friend in need is a friend indeed" mean that (1) a friend who needs something from you is really a friend at that time, or that (2) one who is a friend to you in your time of need is really a friend? In other words, am I, who thinks the first is the common use of that phrase, really more cynical than everyone else at work?

—*Scot B., via the Internet.*

Well, maybe. Proverbs can be tricky little critters. Scores of otherwise compassionate people, for example, believe that "Feed a cold, starve a fever" means that you should simply stop feeding a really sick person. My research indicates that people who interpret "Feed a cold, starve a fever" that way tend to have difficulty maintaining long-term relationships.

"A friend in need is a friend indeed" is a lovely proverb, it rhymes nicely, and unfortunately, no one knows exactly what it means. The proverb itself has been kicking around for a couple of thousand years and crops up in one form or another in nearly every notable quotable's life work somewhere.

There is some evidence that the uncynical interpretation, that a true friend is one who sticks by you in hard times, was the original meaning of the phrase. Some authorities trace the proverb to a Latin saying, "Amicus certa in re incerta cernitur," which means "A sure friend is made known when one is in difficulty."

Another bit of uncertainty, however, revolves around whether the *indeed* in the phrase might not actually have originally been *in deed,* meaning that a true friend actually does something (a deed) to relieve your distress, rather than just keeping you company while you sink.

Proverbs
can be tricky
little critters.

On the other hand, the "dude pretends to be my friend because he wants to borrow my chain saw" interpretation is, without doubt, more prevalent in the cynical, gimme-gimme world of today. So you should be thankful that you work with a group of such old-fashioned, unselfish people.

full monty

Q: We recently had the pleasure of seeing that marvelous British film *The Full Monty*, and our conversation, at Tokyo's oldest British-style pub, of course, turned to the origins of the term. The first explanation that came up centered on the famed British military leader Viscount Bernard Law Montgomery. It seems that during World War II, "Monty" could not go off to battle in the morning without a full English-style breakfast in all its glory. (Something about the infantry traveling on its stomach, perhaps?) Word of this got around and led to the phrase *the full monty* coming to mean "the complete goods" or "the whole deal." The other explanation had to do with one of the finest smokes on this mortal vale of tears (in this humble correspondent's opinion): a Cuban Monte Cristo. After dining on a full-course meal, the male gentry, if they were truly living large, would light up a Monte Cristo as the perfect way to complete the culinary experience. In other words, a really grand dinner was "the full monty." From there, it wasn't too much of a stretch to get that meaning of "complete" or "total." As good as both these explanations sound, is either close?

—*David S., Tokyo, Japan.*

EVAN MORRIS

They do sound good, don't they? You have lucidly set forth the two most commonly cited explanations for *the full monty*. Unfortunately, both stories are almost certainly wrong. *The full monty* only appeared in general usage in Britain in the mid-1980s, far too late to have been common wartime slang, and there is no evidence connecting it to cigars.

There is, however, some evidence to indicate that *the full monty* was originally underworld slang for "the pot, or pool of money, at stake in a card game," which would certainly fit in with its current meaning of "the whole shebang." This *monty* is probably related to an archaic card game called *monte* (Spanish for "mountain"), named for the pile of cards from which players draw, a sense perhaps later transferred to the mountain of money at stake in a busy game. The winner in such a high-stakes game could thus well have been said to have won "the full monty." The card game monte lives on, incidentally, in the form of three-card monte, the classic con game (similar to the shell game) common to urban street corners in the United States.

Originally underworld slang for "the pot, or pool of money, at stake in a card game."

gallivant

Q: My supervisor at work recently accused me (in a joking way) of "gallivanting around" and "malingering" on the job. These sound like your sort of words—where did they come from? —*Vincent F., Queens, New York.*

My sort of words, eh? I think I resent that. As to where they came from, they came from your supervisor—weren't you listening? No wonder you're always in trouble. You'll never make Chief Burger Flipper with an attitude like that.

Gallivant is a fine old word, meaning "to wander around idly, especially with members of the opposite sex," so *gallivanting* in your case translates more or less as "wandering around flirting." No wonder your boss is annoyed. The origins of *gallivanting* are a bit obscure, although it is almost certainly related to *gallant* as a noun, meaning "ladies' man." The late poet and etymologist John Ciardi thought that *gallivant* was actually a combination of the French form of *gallant* and *avant* (to go forward), thus giving us "to go out and play the ladies' man."

Malinger is also a fine old word, but I wonder if that's what your supervisor really meant to say. *Malinger* means "to feign or exaggerate illness in order to avoid work or duty" and comes from the Old French *malingre*, meaning "sickly." *Malingering* does not, as many people seem to think, mean "wasting time" or "dawdling." My guess is that folks hear the word *linger* in there and assume *malinger* is just a fancy way of saying "goofing off." Since it's pretty hard to flirt effectively at the same time one is pretending to be at death's door, your supervisor was probably making this error. Still, I'd clean up my act if I were you—it's hard to gallivant on the unemployment line.

It's hard to GALLIVANT on the unemployment line.

EVAN MORRIS

galoot

Q : Can you tell me where the word *galoot* comes from, as in "Ya big galoot"? I was wondering if it might have originated in the Galeutian Islands (you know, off the coast of Galaska).

—*Jim V., New York, New York.*

Very funny. I can see that we have a discipline problem among readers of this column. Maybe you won't find this pop quiz quite so funny: list ten of my topics from the last six months, excluding anecdotes about my cat. You have fifteen minutes. And you, out there in Wisconsin—spit out that gum.

Galoot, meaning "an awkward or foolish person," is usually only applied to men. Perhaps it's the influence of movies and books (I seem to vaguely remember John Wayne saying "Ya big galoot" in some horse opera or other, and the term occurs in the western novels of Louis L'Amour), but *galoot* has taken on the added connotation of "big, dumb fellow" in the popular vernacular, so it's unlikely you'll hear *galoot* applied to a woman.

It's unlikely you'll hear GALOOT applied to a woman.

Galoot is a mystery—we know roughly where and when it showed up, but not where it came from. Thanks to all those horse operas, most of us associate *galoot* with cowboys, but the term was apparently actually invented by sailors around 1812 and applied to soldiers and marines, most likely those being transported by ship. Although soldiers and marines might well face hardship and danger when they reached their destination, they were not expected to work while aboard ship. Naturally, the sailors resented the soldiers' privileged shipboard status, and the derogatory term *galoot* was probably concocted as a small but satisfying means of revenge. If so, it wasn't the only linguistic jab by the resentful sailors—the slang term *soldier,* meaning "to loaf," originated in the navy at about the same time. On dry land, on the other hand, *to soldier* means "to persevere," most often heard in the phrase *to soldier on.* Not surprisingly, this more positive sense of the term is assumed to have originated in the army.

gaudy

Q: I was recently told that the word *gaudy* comes from the name of the Catalan architect Antoni Gaudí. I find this hard to believe, as he died in the late 1920s, and it seems to me that this word is of older origin. Can you give me more information? —*Janis B., via the Internet.*

Well, there you go. As I've said before, I have the most perceptive readers around. Presented with an explanation of *gaudy* reeking of hogwash, Ms. B. says, politely but firmly, that she finds it "hard to believe." What she really means, of course, is "Get that ridiculous story away from me before I call the cops."

As well she should. Nobody minds a little creative conjec-

GAUDY

Most etymologists doubt that *gaudy-green* was the root of our more generally tasteless, Elvis sort of GAUDY.

ture every so often, but trying to trace a word such as *gaudy,* which has been in common usage since the sixteenth century, to a twentieth-century architect whose name just happens to sound like *gaudy* is a bit much.

That's not to say that there hasn't been a bit of a debate about the origin of *gaudy,* meaning "tastelessly ornate or showy." One theory traces *gaudy* to an old Middle English term, *gaudy-green,* which was evidently a sort of bright yellowish green. Gaudy-green dye was made from the weld plant (*Reseda luteola,* for you botanists out there), whose name in Old French was *gaude,* so that's where gaudy-green got its name, anyway. But most etymologists doubt that *gaudy-green* was the root of our more generally tasteless, Elvis sort of *gaudy.*

A more likely source is the obsolete English word *gaud,* meaning "joke," "toy," or "showy ornament." This *gaud* came from the French *gaudir,* meaning "to rejoice or jest," which came in turn from the Latin *gaudere,* meaning "to rejoice or delight in." (That Latin *gaudere,* by the way, is also the source of the English word *joy.*) With *gaud* already meaning "showy ornament," it would have been a short leap to *gaudy,* meaning "cheaply ornate."

gormless

Q : I know what *gormless* means, but why? Do most people have gorm, to one degree or another? I first heard this word in the context "She's not stupid, she's gormless!"

—*David H., via the Internet.*

Well, yes, most people do have a sizable pile of gorm, and we use it every day. Did you not get yours? Perhaps you have simply mislaid your gorm. Check in the back of your closets. After all, you wouldn't have written to me if you were entirely gormless.

Gormless comes from the old Scots word *gaum,* meaning "attention" or "notice." Someone who is gormless lacks attention, doesn't notice things, is tuned out, vegged out, hopeless, and clueless. Dumber, in other words, than dirt. *Gormless* is chiefly heard in Britain, where it has been used since the seventeenth century. Emily Brontë used the term in *Wuthering Heights.*

Gorm all by itself ought, logically, to mean "intelligence" (as its predecessor *gaum* did), but today it is heard only as a clipped slang form of *gormless.* So if someone calls you a *gorm,* they're calling you an idiot, and it's not a compliment.

Nor, since we're on the general subject of arcane insults, should you send flowers to anyone who calls you *feckless,* another term heard primarily in Britain. *Feckless* also comes to us from Scots. The Scots *feck* is actually an aphesis, or cropping, of the English

If someone calls you a GORM, they're calling you an idiot, and it's not a compliment.

EVAN MORRIS

word *effect.* Someone who is feckless is, therefore, weak or helpless, and ineffective in the extreme. Utterly useless.

In current usage, *feckless* often does duty as a synonym for "aimless" or "irresponsible"—*feckless youth* is a well-worn cliché, but true fecklessness knows no age limit. A lifelong loser who embraces (and tries to enlist others in) one get-rich-quick scheme after another probably qualifies to be called *feckless.* The folks who actually turn over their savings accounts to him, on the other hand, richly deserve the label of *gormless.*

Gotham

Q: Could you please tell me the origin of the word *Gotham.* I know it is used to identify New York City, but why is that, and how did that come about?

—*Don S., via the Internet.*

Ah, New York, New York, the town so nice they named it twice. I really miss living full-time in New York City, although no one out here in Ohio believes me when I say that. But it's true. Sometimes I even lock myself in the hall closet and pretend I'm back in the living room of my apartment on the Upper West Side.

GOTHAM itself passed into legend as the home of wise fools.

The use of *Gotham* as a synonym for New York City goes back quite a ways. Washington Irving, the creator of "The Legend of Sleepy Hollow," first used it to refer to New York in 1807. In his *Salmagundi,* a satirical journal, he depicted Gothamites as wiseacres and know-it-alls, a popular view of New Yorkers that hasn't changed in the intervening years. The question, of course, is why he chose that particular name, *Gotham*.

Cut, as they say in the movie biz, to thirteenth-century England and the real village of Gotham, near Nottingham. According to legend, King John once made a trip to Gotham for the announced purpose of acquiring land and building himself a fine hunting lodge. The villagers, however, had no wish to be taxed to support the king's court and devised a clever plan of action. When the king's advance men rode into Gotham, they found the villagers running wildly in circles and behaving in a thoroughly demented manner. The king, informed that he would be residing among madmen, dropped his plans and took his lodge elsewhere, whereupon the "wise fools" of the village were said to have remarked that "more fools pass through Gotham than remain in it." Gotham itself passed into legend as the home of such wise fools, and surely it was their combination of demented behavior and cunning, the "method in their madness," that led Washington Irving to dub New Yorkers the modern *Gothamites*.

grain of salt

Q: Please help me! I have been looking forever for the origins of the phrase *take that with a grain of salt*. I was hoping you could help. —*Bethany L., via the Internet.*

Well, you've certainly come to the right place: *grain of salt* is my middle name. I am known among my friends, in fact, as Mr. Yeah, Right. It may be unfashionable, but I wear my skepticism with pride. After all, among the most popular television shows at the moment are those devoted to "documenting" UFO abductions, psychic phenomena, and similar postrational twaddle. Of course, I know my faithful readers would never stoop to watching such balderdash. Besides, you're all too busy consulting the *I Ching*, right?

To take something with a grain of salt means "to not entirely believe a story, or to view it with a healthy degree of skepticism." It doesn't mean that you think the person recounting the story is completely crazy or making it all up. It just means you don't want to be close enough to get caught under the net his keepers are fixing to drop on him.

It may be unfashionable, but I wear my skepticism with pride.

It's fitting that you've been looking for the origin of this phrase "forever," because *with a grain of salt* has been around nearly that long. It's actually a translation of the Latin phrase *cum grano salis.* There seems to be a bit of a debate about the significance of the Latin phrase, however. Etymologist Christine Ammer traces it to Pompeii's discovery, recorded by Pliny in A.D. 77, of an antidote to poison that had to be taken with a small amount of salt to be effective.

Most other authorities seem to bypass that explanation and trace *with a grain of salt* to the dinner table, where a dash of salt can often make uninspired cooking more palatable. *With a grain of salt* first appeared in English in 1647 and has been in constant use since then. The amount of salt needed to make an unlikely statement acceptable often varies, metaphorically, from a few grains to a few pounds. With all the flapdoodle being thrust at us these days, I'm surprised there isn't a national salt shortage.

gringo

Q: Please inform us of the origin of the Mexican Spanish derogatory slang term *gringo*. Southwest folklore has it that Black Jack Pershing's boys, sitting around the campfires, would be overheard singing "Green Grow the Lilacs," and the locals soon started calling the Yanks *gringos*.

—*Riley, via the Internet.*

Hold it right there, buckaroo. Derogatory? *Gringo?* Are you sure about that? Holy cow. This casts a whole new light on some of the mail I've been getting from the Southwest. I was under the impression that *gringo* was a laudatory form of address, akin to what my friends tell me it means to be addressed as *schmuck* in Brooklyn. I hope they're not putting me on about that, too.

In any case, what you've heard is just one of several stories purporting to explain the origin of *gringo*, most of which center on the Mexican-American War of the nineteenth century. Another explanation traces the word to the green uniforms supposedly worn by U.S. soldiers, which, again supposedly, prompted the Mexicans to shout, "Green go!" This story falls under the rule that any explanation requiring more than one *supposedly* should not be taken seriously.

The Spanish word GRINGO means "foreigner" or "unintelligible gibberish."

As one of our readers, writing from Mexico in fact, noted a few years ago, both these theories conclusively run aground on the fact that *gringo* crops up in written Spanish quite a while before the war in question—in 1787, to be exact.

The most likely source of our slang meaning of *gringo* is the Spanish word *gringo* itself, which means "foreigner" or "unintelligible gibberish." The root of *gringo,* in turn, is thought to have been *griego,* Spanish for "Greek," often applied as slang to any foreigner. But why, I hear you ask, Greeks? Because the Greek language has long been a convenient metaphor for anything foreign and unintelligible. Even the Romans had a Latin phrase for the feeling of being stymied by the unfamiliar: "Graecum est; non potest legi." Translation? "It is Greek; it cannot be read," or as we say today, "It's Greek to me."

gunnysack

Q: I'm wondering about the origin of the word *gunnysack*. Did it originally mean "a sack for guns"?

—*Meg B., via the Internet.*

Say, I'm no public policy expert, but I think you may have inadvertently stumbled upon a solution to the gun control

You Took the Words Right Out
of My Mouth . . .

Anyone who doubts that food occupies a place of honor in the human imagination need only open a dictionary of slang or common English idioms. Hundreds of our most commonly heard expressions are drawn from the chow line, and more (e.g., "Where's the beef?" of Wendy's commercial and presidential campaign fame) are added every year. Here are a few choice tidbits (*tidbit* means "small tasty morsel," from the English dialect word *tid*, "tender," plus *bit*).

a chicken in every pot: Economic prosperity. A very old metaphor, revived to take center stage as a campaign slogan in the 1928 U.S. presidential election (immediately preceding the Great Depression).

easy as pie: Very easy or simple, since the early twentieth century. Of debatable logic, since making a good pie is anything but easy. May be a mangling of *nice as pie* (very nice), which makes much more sense.

eat humble pie: To apologize and be forced to acknowledge one's errors, since about 1830. This phrase is actually a pun on *umble pie*, a lowly servants' dish made from the *umbles* ("innards," ultimately from the Latin *lumbus,* "loin") of deer, as opposed to the venison their masters ate.

full of beans: Energetic, feisty. (*Feisty* originally meant "flatulent," so the bean connection certainly fits.)

milktoast: An ineffectual or feeble man. Milktoast (toast soaked in milk, sometimes with added butter and sugar) has been fed to toothless infants for centuries and used as a metaphor for wimpiness just as long. Often spelled *Milquetoast* in the United States, after Caspar Milquetoast, a popular old-time comic strip character.

proof of the pudding is in the eating: You can't judge a thing until you put it to its intended use, *proof* in this case meaning "test" or "trial." An old and oft-quoted proverb dating back at least to the seventeenth century.

rhubarb: An uproar or ruckus. Thought to have come from the practice of having extras in theatrical crowd scenes say "Rhubarb" over and over, simulating the sound of an angry mob.

small beer: Inconsequential or trivial. In the sixteenth century, "weak or inferior beer," soon applied to anything not worth worrying about.

sour grapes: Now often taken to mean simply "the bitterness of a sore loser," *sour grapes* originally meant "to disparage as unworthy that which you cannot attain." The phrase comes from Aesop's fable about the fox who, unable to reach the grapes he desired, announced that he didn't want them anyway because he knew that they were sour.

tripe: Nonsense, intellectual rubbish. Tripe is a dish made from the stomach of a cow or sheep, and although it has its partisans, tripe has been a synonym for "worthless" since the seventeenth century. Now usually applied to substandard writing or art.

the world is your oyster: You have endless opportunities. From Shakespeare's *The Merry Wives of Windsor,* wherein a character announces "Why then the world's mine oyster, which I with sword will open" to extract the pearls of wealth within.

debate. Something tells me that gun ownership (at least among men) would drop precipitously if we simply passed a law requiring all firearms, at all times, to be referred to as *gunnies*. Reminds you of fluffy little bunnies, doesn't it? That's the idea. And I'll bet that if we further decreed that gunnies could be purchased only in pastel colors or tasteful floral patterns, we'd render the whole debate moot toot sweet. Of course, then we'd have to keep a close eye on Martha Stewart, but I still think it's worth a try.

Meanwhile, back at your question, no, *gunnysack* has nothing to do with guns. Gunnysacks are, of course, large bags made with very coarse cloth, usually woven from either jute or hemp. Such sacks are (or at least were in the past) often used for packing agricultural products, such as sugar or grain, for shipment. Gunnysacks have been around for a very long time, as you might guess from the fact that *gunny* comes directly from the ancient Sanskrit word *goni,* meaning "sack." The English version *gunny* first appeared around 1711, probably imported from the Hindi by British merchants importing goods from India.

GUNNY comes directly from the ancient Sanskrit word goni, meaning "sack."

Incidentally, and this is very weird, the word *gun,* meaning "firearm," probably comes from a common Scandinavian female name. *Gunnhildr* (which itself is a combination of *gunnr* and *hildr,* both meaning "war") was used as a nickname for rock-hurling catapults in the Middle Ages, much as the largest German artillery pieces during World War I were known as *Big Berthas.* When cannons and small arms came along later, they too were known as *Gunnhildrs* (or the shorter form *Gunnes*), and we've been living with *guns* ever since.

hair of the dog that bit you

Q: I have two questions. First, what is the saying about curing a hangover the next day? Something like *bite the dog's tail* or *the dog that bit you last night?* Second, where does this come from? —*Wiley, via the Internet.*

Wiley, old pal, I want you to try a little experiment for me. I want you to give that "bite the dog's tail" business a shot and get back to me, when you can, with the results. My guess is that your canine therapy will indeed clear your head, but that you may encounter subsequent medical expenses that rule it out as an economically sound solution to hangovers.

Just kidding, of course. Please don't go chewing on old Fido. You'll end up with a mouthful of dog hair, and I'll end up with a mailbox full of outraged reader mail (which is worse, I assure you).

The phrase you're looking for is *hair of the dog that bit you,* and it is a metaphor for the dubious practice of curing a hangover after a night of heavy drinking by simply drinking a bit more of whatever gave you the hangover in the first place. Most medical authorities agree that this method will, at best, simply delay the onset of an even worse hangover. Or you'll end up drunk and hungover simultaneously.

It is a metaphor for the dubious practice of curing a hangover by simply drinking a bit more of whatever gave you the hangover in the first place.

While the hair of the dog that bit you may not work as a hangover cure, the phrase is interesting because it arose as an allusion to an older practice, that of treating dog bites with a poultice containing the hair of the offending dog itself. The use of *hair of the dog that bit you* as a metaphor for curing a hangover with more drink dates back to about 1546, while the practice of actually putting dog hair on bites is much older (and even less effective).

I'm not much of a drinker (the last hangover I had was on New Year's Day 1989), so I don't have many suggestions to make about hangover cures. In the case of my New Year's debacle, chicken soup proved to be an amazingly effective restorative, but then again, chicken soup cures darn near anything, short of a dog bite.

hamburger

Q: Why is hamburger called *hamburger* when it doesn't come from pigs?　　　*—Kendra R., via the Internet.*

But hot dogs do. As we say in New York City, go figure. Speaking of New York City and pigs (which I am determined to do, so you might as well sit back and relax), I have been doing a bit of research on the city's history and have discovered something rather amazing. It seems that until an organized corps of New York City street cleaners was established in the middle of the nineteenth century, public sanitation tasks were handled by twenty thousand "street hogs" that roamed the city freely, snarfing up all the garbage. European visitors were appalled by the spectacle of herds of swine wandering down the fashionable avenues, but the children of the city had great fun chasing and lassoing the critters. I love New York.

I'm not very fond of hamburger, however, since I've always had a soft spot for cows, but I'll try not to let my prejudice flavor my answer to your question. The *ham* in *hamburger* doesn't have anything to do with ham. Hamburgers (originally known as *hamburger steaks*) are so-called because they are thought to have been invented in Hamburg, Germany, although chopping up some lean beef and frying it doesn't seem like a terribly challenging concept, so hamburger was probably actually invented in numerous locales. The original recipe for hamburger steak, by the way, sounds more like meatloaf than hamburgers, involving beaten eggs, spices, and onions. *Hamburger* made its first appearance in English at the end of the nineteenth century.

The popularity of hamburgers has led, on the model of *Watergate/Irangate/Travelgate*, ad nauseam, to a plethora of *burger* compounds. We can now order, among other mutations, cheeseburgers, pizza burgers, soy burgers (ugh), veggie burgers (double ugh), and turkey burgers, which really aren't bad at all. To my knowledge, no one has ever successfully marketed a true ham burger, but such a thing might not be half bad with cheese.

We now have cheeseburgers, pizza burgers, soy burgers (ugh), veggie burgers (double ugh), and turkey burgers.

happy as a clam

Q: The other day, in summarizing the results of a hard day's work taming a computer problem, I used the expression *happy as a clam* to describe the prevailing feeling at having gotten it done. That immediately made me wonder, "Who ever came up with the idea that clams are happy?" (Someone else immediately asked where you'd get clams anyway, this being a city far from any major body of water, but that's another matter.)

—*A. H., via the Internet.*

Try your grocer's freezer, as the commercials say. I actually happen to love frozen fried clams, even though I am fully aware that they would be more accurately labeled *vaguely clam-flavored bits of fried dough*. Then again, I really like McDonald's Filet-O-Fish sandwich, so I may not be the world's most reliable guide to gourmet seafood.

No, the world is not a clam's oyster.

I agree that there is no credible evidence to suggest that clams are, as a rule, happy. In fact, what little scientific research has been done so far in Seafood Studies tends to indicate that clams live out their lives in an advanced state of existential dread, and who can blame them? Not a lot to look forward to in clam world, is there? No little clam books, no clam music, and it wouldn't do a clam one bit of good to win lotto. No, the world is not a clam's oyster.

EVAN MORRIS

Still, as I learned in college, everything is relative. And, relatively speaking, the happiest time of a clam's day is almost certainly high tide, when his sandy abode is safely hidden from the eagle eyes of the dreaded clam diggers who prowl the beaches at low tide. So *happy as a clam* actually does make sense if we use it in its original, complete form, which is *happy as a clam at high tide,* a catchphrase that apparently originated in New England back in the early eighteenth century and has been used ever since to mean "perfectly contented."

Hector

Q: Please advise me of the source of the phrase *since Hector was a pup.* In fact, I myself haven't heard that phrase since I was a pup! —*R. H., Meriden, Connecticut.*

Me neither. Hey, what do you say we bring this saying back? I'll bet that if we all pepper our daily speech with *since Hector was a pup,* we'll have Ted Koppel using it within six months.

Since Hector was a pup is a catchphrase, a popular figure of speech, that has been around at least since the 1920s, when *Hector* was a popular name for dogs. *Since Hector was a pup* is actually a sort of pun, because it refers to both *Hector* as a popular dog's name and another, far older Hector.

The original Hector was a hero in the *Iliad,* the Greek poet Homer's epic narrative of the ten-year war between ancient

Even linguistic immortality can be a double-edged sword.

Greece and Troy. The Trojan War began when Paris, son of the Trojan king Priam, ran off with Helen, wife of the Greek king of Sparta. Hector was Paris's brother and in Homer's account a brave and noble fellow, just the sort you'd name your dog after if you had read the *Iliad* in school (which was much more likely in the 1920s). In any event, the Trojan War is reckoned to have taken place in about 1200 B.C., so the original Hector was a "pup," a young man, a very long time ago.

Even though he was ultimately slain by the Greek hero Achilles, Hector of Troy lives on in another form, as an English verb. Since the seventeenth century, *hector* has meant "to harass and bully," which is rather odd, considering what a nice guy Hector is supposed to have been. Hector's modern image problem probably began when seventeenth-century pundits said of their local bully, "He must think he's Hector, hero of Troy," the way we might say "Oh boy, here comes Superman" today. So the saga of poor Hector proves that even linguistic immortality can be a double-edged sword.

hello

Q: Where did the word *hello* come from? I read somewhere that Alexander Graham Bell invented it, along with the telephone, but isn't it much older than that?

— Susan D., New York, New York.

EVAN MORRIS

There may be English words we use more frequently than *hello,* but not many. Almost every social encounter begins with it, and unless you answer the phone "Big Al's World o' Ribs," you probably say, "Hello." There are exceptions, of course. I had an acquaintance a few years back who routinely answered the telephone by saying, "Telephone," which made a certain weird sense but often led to long silences at the other end of the line.

One of the absolutely certain things we can say about *hello* is that Alexander Graham Bell did not invent it. In fact, Bell resolutely refused to answer the phone with *hello,* supposedly because his archrival, Thomas Alva Edison, had been responsible for popularizing the practice. Bell preferred to answer his phone by saying, "Ahoy," which works if you're a famous inventor but probably wouldn't go over well in most modern offices.

Bell preferred to answer his phone by saying, "Ahoy," which works if you're a famous inventor but probably wouldn't go over well in most modern offices.

As a matter of fact, *hello* antedates the telephone by several centuries. Folks in Chaucer's time greeted each other with *hallow,* which may have come from the Old French *hola,* meaning essentially "stop!" or "whoa!" By the time the telephone came along, Americans were saying *hullo,* so it was a short jump to *hello.*

As a telephone greeting, *hello* now seems to be nearly worldwide. A few years ago I dialed a long-distance call to what I thought was Connecticut, but the man who answered the phone spoke no English beyond *hello.* This in itself would not be terribly surprising in the United States, but when I received my phone bill, I found that I had inadvertently discovered yet another place where they answer the telephone with *hello*—Cairo, Egypt.

hoosegow

Q: My bubee and I find ourselves using the word *hooscow* frequently. We live near Dallas, and with all those Dallas Cowboys being "boys," we have cause to use this word a lot. Of course, I'm talking about jail. Not sure on the spelling but thought you would know what I mean. Any help, please?

—Cathy S., via the Internet.

You are a bit off on the spelling—it is *hoosegow*—but you're using the right word for your part of the country. *Hoosegow* comes from the Mexican Spanish word *juzgado,* meaning "tribunal" or "judge." Originally the juzgado was the local courthouse in the Old West, but frontier justice being what it was, *jail* was a functional synonym, and the English version *hoosegow* never meant anything but "the clink." The same word *juzgado* also gave us *jug* as a term for jail. The ultimate root of *juzgado,* by the way, is the Latin *judicare,* meaning "to judge," which also gave us *judicial* and *judgment,* among other words. Interestingly enough (to me, at least), although we can assume *hoosegow* is a genuine Old West word used in the nineteenth century, the earliest written example yet found is from much later, in 1911. I guess those cowboys just didn't understand how important precise documentation of their slang would be someday.

There must be something about the prospect of jail that sets the old slang machine to humming, incidentally, because English has some very colorful terms for "the pokey" (from *poke*, a nineteenth-century term meaning "to confine"). Along with *the clink* (originally the actual name of a famous English prison, possibly derived from the sound a closing jail cell door makes), we have *the can, the tank, the slammer, the cooler, the joint, lockup,* and *the big house,* among others. And yet another Spanish word, *calabozo* (dungeon) lives on today as *calaboose.*

I guess those cowboys just didn't understand how important precise documentation of their slang would be someday.

hullabaloo

Q: I am a junior at Tulane University in New Orleans. Our school newspaper is called the *Hullabaloo,* and I believe the paper is named from the school cheer: "One, two, a helluva hullabaloo, a hullabaloo ray-ray, a hullabaloo ray-ray, tee-ay, tee-ay, vars-vars tee-ay, tee-ay tee-ay Tulane!" That was a fun song to learn as a freshman! I have seen various TV shows (e.g., *The Simpsons*) use *hullabaloo,* and it makes me wonder where Tulane got the word. — *Chad C., via the Internet.*

Well, Chad, that may have been a fun song to learn as a freshman, but I must warn you that your school's little ditty may now linger with you for life and pop into your noggin at the most inopportune moments imaginable. I remember contracting food poisoning a few years ago and being plagued throughout my ordeal by a mental tape loop of my old school song, "Boys of Brunswick," a ghastly (albeit unintentional) parody of the heroic Welsh song "Men of Harlech." And they wonder why I don't come to reunions.

The basic meaning of *hullabaloo* is "a noise or clamor, a scene of uproar or confusion," and it's often used as a loose synonym for "ruckus." The first written occurrence of *hullabaloo* found so far was back in 1762, when it was spelled *hollo-ballo.* (Other forms have included *halaballoo, hilliebalow,* and endless variations on that theme.) *Hullabaloo* apparently entered English from either Scots or northern English dialects.

Hullo was sometimes repeated with a slight variation, in a process linguists call reduplication, to produce hullo bullo.

No one knows exactly where *hullabaloo* came from, but there's a good chance that it all started with the exclamation *hullo* (used to get someone's attention, and the ancestor of our modern *hello*), which was often repeated to indicate surprise or excitement. The classic British policeman's exclamation of "Allo, allo, what's going on 'ere?" is an example of this repetitive use. *Hullo* was also sometimes repeated with a slight variation, in a process linguists call reduplication, to produce *hullo bullo* and its cousins, which more than likely became *hullabaloo.*

humongous

Q : Can you tell us the origin of the word *humongous?* Was it by chance invented by a little girl in the early fifties to describe the Grand Canyon?

—Anonymous, via the Internet.

Yes, it was, in 1954 to be exact. Fortunately, the little girl's daddy just happened to be an attorney, and he had the foresight to trot back to Washington right away and register *humongous* as a trademark. And that, dear reader, is why you owe "Little Debbie" Furshlinger (now in her late forties, actually) of Des Moines $428.76 for using *humongous* in your question. And if you think that "anonymous e-mail" business will save you, you haven't met many trademark lawyers.

I'm just kidding, of course. *Humongous* isn't trademarked, although it's a bit surprising that somebody hasn't tried to legally claim it as their personal property. After all, just a few years ago *Wired* magazine was running around trying to sue anyone who so much as mumbled the word *wired* in their sleep, notwithstanding the fact that *wired* has been in use since around A.D. 1413.

In any case, the story you've heard is probably not true, and the true inventor of *humongous* (sometimes spelled *humungous*), slang meaning "huge" or

Experts believe that it was probably coined as a humorous combination of *huge* and *monstrous* with a little bit of *tremendous* thrown in.

"tremendous," will probably remain a mystery forever. We do know that *humongous* first showed up in print around 1968 as college slang. Experts believe that it was probably coined as a humorous combination of *huge* and *monstrous* with a little bit of *tremendous* thrown in. This sort of invention is not uncommon in slang. A similar word also dating back to the 1960s, *gigunda,* was almost certainly a silly modification of *gigantic,* and the venerable *bodacious* was probably coined by some nineteenth-century wag combining *bold* and *audacious.*

Idaho

Q: I think this will probably be an easy one. From where does the state name *Idaho* come? And while I'm at it, I might as well ask what the acronym *ACME* means.

—J. S., Everett, Washington, via the Internet.

An easy one, eh? Not so fast, friend. I know when I'm being set up. Since you live in Washington State, you know darn well that there's no such place as Idaho. This so-called state was invented by eighteenth-century American mapmakers too lazy to bother with anything beyond Indiana. Even after Walt Disney discovered California, cartographers continued to label a great unexplored patch of America's Northwest *Idaho.* But think about it for a moment—an entire state devoted to raising potatoes? Does that really sound plausible?

Oh, all right, since you're serious, here you go. *Idaho* comes from *Idahi,* which is what the Kiowa Apache tribe called their Comanche neighbors. Curiously enough, *Idaho* was first proposed as a name for what is now the state of Colorado. On the other hand, for some reason, folks originally wanted to call Idaho *Montana.* Got that? Colorado was going to be called *Idaho,* and Idaho was going to be called *Montana.* So, do you still believe in Idaho?

Think about it for a moment— an entire state devoted to raising potatoes? Does that really sound plausible?

I'm not sure what, if anything, *acme* has to do with Idaho (the state motto of which is "Esta Perpetua," meaning "It is forever," an odd motto for a state that doesn't exist in the first place), but I can tell you that *acme* is not an acronym. It comes from the Greek word *akme,* meaning "highest point" or "summit." Many companies used to name themselves *Acme Widgets* or the like as a means to ensure that they would appear near the beginning of any alphabetical listing. Eventually, so many companies tried this trick that *Acme* in a corporate name came to be regarded as a bit of a joke and was replaced by more dignified names, such as *Burger King* and *Toys "R" Us.* So much for progress. It's enough to make me want to move to Idaho.

idiosyncrasy

Q: My significant other and I are having a discussion about the meaning and etymology of the word *idiosyncrasy.* Can you offer some insight into this? I was attempting to explain what I felt the word meant by breaking it down into its root parts. These seemed to me to be *idio,* meaning "one's individual self," and *sync,* meaning "coordinated" or "meshing" (as in synchronous computer communications or synchronized swimming, etc.).   *—Mark C., via the Internet.*

Far be it from my place to buck the tide of social progress as reflected in the sometimes murky mirror of our language, but I simply must take this opportunity to note that the term *significant other* has always given me significant whim-whams. Aside from the somewhat tepid connotations of *significant* in a romantic context ("Marry me, darling. You're significant to me"), every time I hear the phrase, I wonder whether I've fallen in with someone harboring multiple personalities ("Well, yes, there are many of me, but Sybil is my most significant other").

Now that I've put a dent in your relationship with your sweetie, please accept my congratulations—you are definitely on the right track about *idiosyncrasy.* The Greek root *idio* does indeed mean "of a particular person" or "personal" and crops up

Idiot comes from the same Greek root, originally simply meaning "common man" and only much later coming to mean "television newscaster."

in many other English words, such as *idiom,* "one's own way of speaking." *Idiot* comes from the same Greek root, originally simply meaning "common man" and only much later coming to mean "television newscaster."

You're essentially right about the *sync* part, too. The Greek root was *synkrasis,* meaning "a blending or mixture," or, as you put it, a "meshing." Put all the pieces together, and we have *idiosyncrasy,* meaning "an individual's mixture of personal characteristics."

Incidentally, *idiosyncrasy* is one of those rare English words whose modern sense corresponds almost precisely to the combined meanings of its ancient roots. Language almost never operates in such an orderly fashion, and it is far more common to find that the roots of a word bear only a tangential logical relation to its current meaning.

jackpot

Q: I am in search of the roots of the phrase *hit the jackpot.* What was the first jackpot?

—*Michael D., via the Internet.*

The first jackpot? Why, that would be the ill-fated Great Babylonian Pottery Lottery of 420 B.C., in which the first prize was six hundred pickled sheep packed into an enormous urn ninety Crullers (about seventy feet) tall. I understand they're still trying to catch up with the winner.

Lotteries today are far more successful, of course, at least for those who run them. My favorite is the multistate Powerball lottery, where your chances of hitting the jackpot are statistically so remote that you are just as likely to win if you don't buy a ticket in the first place. That's my kind of lottery—the kind I can sleep through.

But *jackpot*, meaning "a large prize in a gambling contest" (or "a great stroke of luck" generally) doesn't come from lotteries. The term actually comes from the world of "serious" gambling, in this case the game of draw poker. Now, before I get too far into this explanation, I should cop to being a poker illiterate. The truth is that I get confused playing go fish. But apparently in certain breeds of draw poker, nobody can start bidding until someone is dealt two jacks. If no one gets two jacks, the cards are shuffled and dealt again. Don't ask me why; it seems like a silly rule, but there it is.

Now the important aspect of this "two jacks" business is that before each deal, each player must ante up a certain sum into the communal pot of money that will go to the eventual winner. If jacks prove elusive through the course of several deals, this pot can grow quite large, and there's your *jackpot*.

Jackpot first appeared in the literal poker sense around 1881 and almost immediately took on the figurative sense of "big prize" or "very good luck" that we know today.

The truth is
that I get confused
playing go fish.

jeep

Q: I am currently engaged in an argument with my father-in-law over the origin of the word *jeep*. He says it is a kind of Turkish land fowl, like, well, a turkey. I say it started with the odd animal with the radar-tail from the old "Popeye" cartoons (such animal, by the way, whose sole noise emanation was, in fact, "Jeep!"). Could you please do some dirty work for me and get the goods on this weird word?

— *Scott H., via the Internet.*

Yeah, sure, I'll do the dirty work for you. That's what I'm here for. In fact, I'd say that most of the readers who write in with questions are trying to win some sort of argument with their mother-in-law, sister, husband, or boss or the Internal Revenue Service. Of course, after I pronounce my verdict, no one worries about the fallout for little old me. But think about it: would you want an entire nation of fathers-in-law ticked off at you because you shot down their pet theory about *cocktail* or *the whole nine yards?* I think you folks should at least chip in on an insurance policy for me.

In this case, however, I may be able to mollify your father-in-law by saying that his "Turkish land fowl" theory of the origin of *jeep* definitely wins the prize for the most unusual and intriguing explanation for a common word I've heard this year. Turkeys aren't from Turkey, incidentally. I know nobody asked,

Nothin' but a Hound Dog

Much has been written about the role of dogs in human society, but remarkably little has been noted about the role dogs play in human writing, or attempts at it. This is a serious oversight. My own two dogs, Brownie and Pokey, to pick a random example, serve a vital function in my daily writing routine. Their task on a typical morning, while I am staring blankly at my computer screen and contemplating a new career in home roofing sales, is to maintain a vigilant watch on my homestead from the window of my office. And they do a bang-up job of it. Let a single, presumably malevolent, sparrow land on the front lawn, a larcenous chipmunk cough quietly in the shrubbery, or any wandering passenger aircraft approach within twenty nautical miles, and I can rest assured that Brownie and Pokey will instantly spring into action and loose a prolonged fusillade of frenzied barking audible three counties away. This little drama occurs rarely, only every ten minutes or so, but I find it immensely helpful. After all, were it not for such interludes, I would doubtlessly produce far too much prose of coherence and charm, become wealthy and famous, and thus run the risk of contracting gout on the Côte d'Azure. Man's best friend, no doubt about it.

English depends on canines for hundreds of its most vivid metaphors and figures of speech. Here is a sampling.

dog days: The hottest days of summer. The Romans, who had neither air-conditioning nor Doppler weather radar, believed that the stifling heat of midsummer was due to the ascendancy of the star Sirius, which they knew as the *Dog Star*. They called this period *dies caniculares,* or "the dog days," a term that appeared in English around 1538.

dog in the manger: An unpleasant person who will not let another have or use something, even though he himself has no use for it. From Aesop's fable about a dog who would not let a horse and ox eat the hay in a manger despite his own distaste for hay. First appeared in the metaphorical sense in the sixteenth century.

dog's breakfast: A mess, a botched job, since the 1930s. Perhaps originally referring to a cooking mishap rendering results fit only for canine consumption.

my dogs are barking: My feet are killing me. The use of *dogs* as slang for "feet" comes from Cockney rhyming slang, the argot of the London underworld in the nineteenth and early twentieth centuries. In rhyming slang, one or two words stand for the "real" word; thus *dog's meat* stood for "feet." Shortened to simply *dogs,* the term is first found in print in a 1924 P. G. Wodehouse story.

putting on the dog: To dress up and make a show of your finery and sophistication. *Dog* was American college slang for "style" in the late nineteenth century, and *to put on the dog* originally meant to dress "ostentatiously or put on airs." It may actually have begun as a reference to the pampered lapdogs then (as now) often kept as companions by women in high society.

shaggy-dog story: A long, meandering, pointless joke involving a voluminous catalog of details and possessing no real punch line; a story that amuses only the teller, who has made his audience wait so long for nothing. The term appeared in the 1940s, named (supposedly) for a rash of such jokes making the rounds at the time featuring a shaggy dog.

yellow dog: A mongrel, cur, or other no-account type of dog, since the eighteenth century, apparently based on the observation (true or not) that nonpedigreed dogs tend to be yellow. *Yellow dog* has been used as slang for "a contemptible human being" since the late nineteenth century, specifically a worker who is opposed to trade unionism. Such a worker would be likely to sign what is called a *yellow-dog contract,* forbidding union membership.

The word JEEP
definitely came
from the name
of the character
Eugene the
Jeep, introduced
in the "Popeye"
comic strip in
1936.

but I thought I'd throw that in. They were dubbed that by confusion with Turkey-cocks, game birds that actually came from Turkish colonies in Africa.

Anyway, your father-in-law is wrong about *jeep,* and you are right, sort of. The word *jeep* definitely came from the name of the character Eugene the Jeep, introduced in the "Popeye" comic strip in 1936. The association of *jeep* with the small four-wheel-drive vehicle, however, wasn't made until a few years later. The army designated these sturdy little trucks *general purpose,* or *GP* for short. To soldiers raised on "Popeye," the transformation of *GP* into *jeep* was inevitable and became so pervasive that Willys-Overland Motors trademarked the name *Jeep* in 1940.

jingo

Q: A spate of recent war talk in the media brought the word *jingoists* to mind. My dictionary tells me it's from a British political song supporting the use of force in Russia in 1878. Clear enough, except who is this Jingo? And why should he become a label for what we now call *hawks?* Can you explain further, or should we send in the troops?

—*Barney J., De Pere, Wisconsin.*

No, you can tell the troops to go sit down. Most people don't know this (and those who do are busy trying to forget), but I am the inventor of the world's first Grammar-Based Defensive Confusion System (GBDCS). Should our country ever be invaded, my GBDCS will spring into action and automatically switch each and every *that* in print in North America to *which* (and vice versa). This diabolical trick will embroil the invaders in endless grammatical squabbles among themselves, rendering them, if not utterly powerless, at least very, very tired.

It's appropriate, given the hall-of-mirrors quality (some would say "smoke and mirrors") of modern politics, that the term *jingo* should have begun life as a magician's incantation. The earliest written instances of *jingo* (around 1670) report it as an exclamation routinely used by conjurers who shouted "Hey jingo!" when making an object appear (as opposed to "Hey presto!" when they made something vanish). *Jingo* probably arose as a euphemism for *Jesus,* much as *gosh* and *golly* started out as substitutes for *God.* The expression *by jingo* was very popular from the seventeenth through the nineteenth centuries.

The "superpatriot" sense of *jingo* does indeed date back to the British-Russian confrontation over Turkey in 1878. A popular British music hall anthem of the day penned by G. W. Hunt declared: "We don't want to fight, yet by Jingo! if we do, we've got the ships, we've got the men, and got the money too!" Those favoring a war with Russia (which was, fortunately, avoided) became known as the *Jingoes,* and the term *jingo* has ever since been a synonym for "a blustering, bellicose patriot."

JINGO probably arose as a euphemism for Jesus, much as gosh and golly started out as substitutes for God.

jumbi

Q : A friend of mine is reading *The Cay* by Theodore Taylor and came across the word *jumbi*. He believes it is related to voodoo. Who or what is a jumbi? Where does the word come from? Or is it like Shangri-La, created by the author to fit the story? —*Judy L., via the Internet.*

Wait just a minute here. If you're implying that Shangri-La is made up, fictional, imaginary, indeed flat-out nonexistent, then I beg to differ with you. Sure, James Hilton swore that he invented Shangri-La, a wondrous paradise hidden deep in the Himalayas, for his 1933 novel *Lost Horizon*. But that's just because he didn't want Tibetan real-estate values to drop like a rock once his novel hit the shelves. I mean, c'mon, given a choice between New Jersey and Shangri-La, people are gonna choose Shangri-La, and then what do you end up with? New Jersey in the Himalayas, that's what. I'm just glad Hilton knew how to keep a secret.

I mean, c'mon, given a choice between New Jersey and Shangri-La, people are gonna choose Shangri-La.

Meanwhile, back at your question, *jumbi* had me stumped for a while, but only as long as it took me to unearth my handy-dandy *Oxford English Dictionary* from beneath the pile of rubble I call my study. According to the *OED, jumbi* (also spelled *jumby* and *jumbee,* among other variations) is a West Indian word for "ghost" or "evil spirit," based on the Kongo word *zumbi,* meaning "charm" or "fetish."

A very old copy of the *Funk & Wagnalls Standard Dictionary of Folklore, Mythology, and Legend* (a marvelous two-volume set that I inherited from my father) adds that jumbies are usually the spirits of dead people that haunt the forests of Caribbean islands, and that the term may be related to the Haitian word *zombi,* or what every horror-movie aficionado knows as *zombies.*

And now I hope you're satisfied, because just typing the answer to your question has given me a bad case of the willies. Thank heavens I've got the weekend to soothe my nerves at my cabin in Shangri-La.

kangaroo court

Q: I am seeking info on the origin of the phrase *kangaroo court.* Various dictionaries have the meaning, but the only etymology I've found is "perhaps by analogy to irregular bounding gait of the animal." That sounds lame to me. How about you?   —*Paul T., via the Internet.*

It sounds lame to me, too, but unfortunately that lameness doesn't rule out the possibility that it's true. In fact, I'm beginning to think that reality as a whole is pretty darn lame, not at all exciting like that groovy *X-Files* stuff. Lately I've resorted to creating my own crop circles and abducting myself for a day or two at a time, but it's no fun playing alone. Maybe I should start a word-origin cult.

One of the strangest aspects of *kangaroo court* is that the phrase is not originally from Australia, which is the only place you'll find actual kangaroos. The first kangaroo courts were informal tribunals set up to dispense instant justice in the American West in the 1850s, before conventional court systems existed on the frontier. Later on, *kangaroo court* was used to describe mock courts set up by penitentiary prisoners to intimidate and extort money from new inmates. Today we usually use the term to mean "any court whose verdict is arranged in advance or otherwise clearly unfair."

The phrase is not originally from Australia.

So the question is why *kangaroo* was used to describe such mockeries of justice, and there are two basic possibilities. First, and most likely, is the theory you mention: that *kangaroo* draws a sardonic analogy between the hopping gait of a kangaroo and the irrational and unpredictable conduct of the original frontier tribunals. Considering the leaps of logic and complete disregard for legal procedure likely to be found in such a proceeding, the comparison certainly seems apt.

Another possibility is that *kangaroo* in this case is simply a metaphor for something utterly alien and unnatural. Remember, there was no Nature Channel or zoos in the Old West. Most people had never even heard of kangaroos, let alone seen one in person, and the critters were generally considered to violate the laws of nature. So labeling something *kangaroo* back then was roughly equivalent to calling it *abnormal* or *bizarre* today, a description that certainly fit the kangaroo courts of the Old West.

EVAN MORRIS

kibosh

Q: Recently a friend of mine used the word *kabosh,* as in "things were going well, and then suddenly the kabosh was on and things weren't going so well." What can you tell me about the origins of this word?

—Jan N., via the Internet.

Well, part of the mystery here lies in the fact that your friend seems to have slightly mispronounced the word, which would make it difficult for you to look it up. What he or she means is *kibosh,* usually pronounced "KYE-bosh."

Kibosh is rarely used these days, so when I hear the word, I immediately think back to the old Bowery Boys comedies of the 1940s, in which Leo Gorcey would often complain of someone "puttin' the kibosh" on the group's plans. He meant, of course, that their plans were stymied or frustrated, *kibosh* being a synonym for "roadblock."

Kibosh is slang, and very old slang indeed— Charles Dickens used it in his description of the squalid sections of London in 1836, although he spelled it *kye-bosk.* Several authorities trace *kibosh* to the Yiddish words *kye* (meaning "eighteen") and *bosh* (meaning "pence"), making a kibosh a coin worth a shilling and sixpence, a negligible sum. Thus, if you

> When I hear the word, I immediately think back to the old Bowery Boys comedies of the 1940s, in which Leo Gorcey would often complain of someone "puttin' the KIBOSH" on the group's plans.

were kiboshed, you were reduced to nearly nothing. Incidentally, the word *bosh,* meaning "nonsense," is not related and comes from the Turkish word *bosh,* meaning "empty" or "worthless."

Another, and more likely, theory is about as far from eighteen pence as you can get. Many authorities believe that *kibosh* was based on the Gaelic phrase *cie báis* (pronounced "ky-bosh"), meaning "cap of death." Evidently, in trials in ancient Ireland, the cie báis, a black skullcap, was donned by the judge before he sentenced a prisoner to death, and apparently the phrase *cie báis* is an established metaphor in modern Irish. An added bit of evidence for this theory is that the Irish term is most often used in the phrase *put the cie báis on,* meaning in Dublin just what *kibosh* meant to the Bowery Boys—"end of story."

kit and caboodle

Q: We were wondering about the origin of *kit and kabootle* (or however you spell it) as it refers to "everything" or "all of it." —*Dave, via the Internet.*

Perhaps it's because I grew up with abnormally fertile cats (I distinctly remember our having nineteen felines of various vintages at one point), but throughout my childhood I blithely assumed that the phrase you're asking about was *kitten caboodle.* I guess it made sense at the time that *caboodle* would be the technical term applied to a group of nine or ten kittens simultaneously climbing lace curtains. Now, of course,

I know that the proper collective term is a *terror* of kittens.

Kit and caboodle (which is the most common form) dates back to the mid–eighteenth century and appeared first in England. There are a number of variants, including *kit and kerboodle* and *kit and boodle*. The *kit* part of the phrase is of fairly straightforward origin, *kit* being an eighteenth-century English slang term for "outfit" or "collection," as in a soldier's *kit bag,* which contained all his worldly possessions. *Kit* may have come from *kith,* meaning "estate," found today in the phrase *kith and kin.*

Caboodle (or *kerboodle,* or just plain *boodle*) is a tougher nut to crack. As usual, there are a number of theories, the most likely of which traces *boodle* back to the Dutch word *boedel,* meaning "property." Lawyers take note: *boodle* was actually a respectable word in its own right (meaning "estate") in the seventeenth and eighteenth centuries and was even used in legal documents. But why *caboodle* or *kerboodle?* The *ca* and *ker* may be related to the intensive German prefix *ge-,* giving the sense "the whole boodle." Put it all together and you get *kit and caboodle,* meaning "everything and all of everything," down to the last kitten.

Incidentally, before I'm buried under an avalanche of mail from agitated animal lovers, let me say that I now understand the importance of neutering one's pets. Both of my present cats, although I haven't had the heart to tell them so, are destined to be without progeny.

Boodle was actually a respectable word in its own right (meaning "estate") in the seventeenth and eighteenth centuries and was even used in legal documents.

lame duck

Q : Do you know the source of the phrase *lame duck?*
—*Barb B., Spokane, Washington.*

Now here's an easy one. The phrase *lame duck* comes to us from Aesop's fables, specifically the tale of Androcles and the duck. It seems that an escaped slave named Androcles encountered a ferocious duck in the forest. But rather than eating the terrified slave, the duck merely asked Androcles to pull a thorn, which was making him lame, from his foot. Androcles complied, and he and the duck became good pals, frequenting local bars and often sharing a cab home.

Many years later, Androcles found himself at a banquet where the main course was roast duck. (Aesop, of course, is best known as the founder of the school of Greek philosophy known as Cheap Irony.) Unable to stomach the thought that his old feathered friend might be, shall we say, integral to the repast, Androcles decided to leave the banquet, but on his way out he accidentally stepped on a lion's paw and was summarily eaten. The moral? Eat what you're served, and never share a cab with a duck.

Aesop, of course, is best known as the founder of the school of Greek philosophy known as Cheap Irony.

Oh, all right, none of that is true. A lame duck (I suppose I ought to call it *flight-challenged*) is one that is unable to keep up with the flock and is thus easy prey for predators. The phrase *lame duck* was first applied on the London Stock Exchange in the eighteenth century to brokers who could not pay their debts. Beginning in nineteenth-century America, *lame duck* was used to describe a congressional representative who had failed to hornswoggle the voters into re-electing him in November, but who was not due, under the Constitution, to actually be booted out until the following March. Thus freed of even the pretense of accountability to the voters, such lame ducks usually voted themselves a scandalous jackpot of perks, until the Lame Duck Amendment of 1934 put a stop to the practice. Today, new members of Congress take office in January, their defeated opponents no longer have an opportunity to loot and pillage on their way out, and thus Congress has become a temple of honesty. And you thought the duck story was ridiculous.

lead-pipe cinch

Q: O.K., it's driving me crazy. I'm a transplant to the Midwest, and the people around here have not heard of the phrase *lead-pipe cinch.* Could you please tell me the origin of this saying?   —*Frustrated in Missouri.*

Tell those people they're watching too much TV. There's actually a bit of a mystery about the origin of *lead-pipe cinch,* which first appeared around 1898, meaning "a sure thing" or "a done deal." The *cinch* part of the phrase seems obvious. A cinch is the strap that holds a saddle securely atop a horse, and thus *cinch* makes a good metaphor for something on which we have a firm grip. *Cinch* used in this sense of "certainty" first appeared around 1888.

The *lead-pipe* part, however, is a little less clear. My initial hunch was that it most likely came from the slang of the criminal underworld, where, in the days before guns were a dime a dozen, a lead pipe was often the most effective means to ensure cooperation. After all, with a lead pipe to back up your wishes, almost anything becomes a cinch.

After I covered this question a number of years ago, two of my readers e-mailed me to explain that in old-fashioned plumbing, short lengths of lead pipe were often used to cinch, or join, longer pipes and fixtures. The lead pipe, being soft, could be tightened around the connecting fixtures, providing a durable and leakproof seal. It was simple yet effective; therefore *lead-pipe cinch* became a metaphor for any easy certainty. I now lean toward this theory.

With a lead pipe to back up your wishes, almost anything becomes a cinch.

Probably the most bizarre theory I've heard about *lead-pipe cinch* traces the phrase to the process of saddling a horse that does not wish to be saddled. Such horses often blow themselves out, or distend their bellies, making cinching the saddle difficult. A lead or steel pipe, goes this theory, was used to tighten the cinch like a tourniquet. Several experienced horse owners have assured me that this is neither a humane nor an effective way to cinch an uppity horse. And it doesn't sound like a lead-pipe cinch, either.

level playing field

Q : I am intrigued by the clichéd expression for equality in opportunity: "All we want is a level playing field." Well, I have never seen a level playing field. Certainly a baseball field is not only not level, but not all have the same measurements; a natural grass football field is not level; a soccer field is not level. Where is the challenge if you play on a nonexistent level playing field? It is a "non-sense" phrase.

—*Larry H., via the Internet.*

Larry, Larry, Larry, what are we gonna do with you? We've got magazine writers, TV commentators, and political speechwriters all working their tiny little brains to a nubbin just to come up with snazzy new metaphors, and what do you do? You pick them apart until there are little bits of cliché all over the rug. What a mess.

Of course there's no such thing as an absolutely perfectly level playing field. And of course, on the other hand, most playing fields are more or less level, and no one plays soccer or baseball on the side of a hill, for gosh sakes.

But *level playing field* isn't supposed to be taken literally. It's a phrase invented in the late 1970s by business theorists who needed a graphic metaphor for equality in the marketplace. Play along for a minute,

You wanna wonder about something? Wonder about Ted Koppel's hair.

O.K.? Just try to imagine how horribly unfair it would be if there really were such things as unlevel playing fields, and your team were looking uphill at the Dallas Cowboys. Now try to imagine what would happen if the free market were actually allowed to run free and certain industries didn't get favorable regulations and government subsidies. Same thing, right? See what I mean?

Reality has nothing to do with it, Larry. It's all public relations. Look, *Nightline* is coming on in a minute. You wanna wonder about something? Wonder about Ted Koppel's hair.

lobster shift

Q: I work the late shift, starting at midnight, and have noticed that all my co-workers call this either the *graveyard shift* or the *lobster shift*. Where did these strange terms come from? —*Don R., New York, New York.*

You certainly have my sympathy—I've never worked the lobster shift, but I have worked late-evening shifts in my long and varied career. Although I looked forward at first to having my days entirely free, what I didn't foresee was that I'd be spending them lost in a catatonic funk of chronic exhaustion. Now that I've brightened your day (night?) with my reminiscences, onward to your question.

Most authorities agree that *graveyard shift* arose from the spookiness of working the "ghostly" hours after midnight, perhaps in a nearly deserted factory with only a "skeletal" crew on duty.

Where *lobster shift* came from is the subject of a number of theories, most of which revolve around the newspaper business in the 1890s. One legend has it that New York City newspapermen on the graveyard shift often stopped at seafood restaurants for dinner on the way to work. Another version, popular in New England, says that the late-shift newspaper workers were going to work at the same time as the lobster boats were setting out to sea.

Yet another, less complimentary, legend alleges that newspapermen on the late shift were habitual drunkards. Supposedly it was their bright red faces, resembling boiled lobsters, that gave the shift its name.

As slanderous to the news profession as that story might be, the most likely contender for the true origin isn't much better. At the turn of the last century, *lobster* was a popular term of derision, meaning "sucker" or "fool," rather like our current *turkey*. Any journalist who found himself snookered into working in the wee hours was likely to earn the derisive title of *lobster* from his day-shift counterparts.

At the turn of the last century, LOBSTER was a popular term of derision, meaning "sucker" or "fool," rather like our current *turkey*.

lukewarm

Q: Could you assist me in finding the origins of *lukewarm,* and perhaps who it was named after?

—*Ingrid Z., via the Internet.*

Why, sure. *Lukewarm* means "barely warm at all," and thereby hangs a tale. Those of us who live in apartment buildings know, of course, that *Luke* is a generic nickname for the building superintendent. It is his job to ensure that your apartment is always at least slightly chilly in the winter and that the temperature of your Monday morning shower never rises above a cozy forty-two degrees Fahrenheit. The Luke in charge of my building, in a perversely brilliant feat of engineering, has managed to make my study the only room in the apartment that has any heat at all for months at a time in the winter. I have reason to believe that he arranged it this way because he knows perfectly well that the whimpering of my wife and two cats outside my study door makes it devilishly hard for me to get any work done.

Of course, the actual origin of *lukewarm* predates apartment buildings, superintendents, and thermostats by quite a bit. *Luke* was an Middle English word, now obsolete, meaning "warm," which was based on *lew,* another word for "warm." *Lew,* in turn, was derived from the Old English word *hleow,* meaning (guess what?) "warm." I guess we can assume that staying warm must have been a major concern of people who

> LUKEWARM actually amounts to saying "warm-warm," but this sort of redundancy is common when obsolete words are carried over into modern usage.

EVAN MORRIS

spoke Old and Middle English. You have probably realized by now that *lukewarm* actually amounts to saying "warm-warm," but this sort of redundancy is common when obsolete words are carried over into modern usage.

If we trace *hleow* back a bit further, we find the Latin word *calor,* meaning "heat." *Calor* gave us *calorie* (a measure of heat), *cauldron,* and, from the derivative word *calere* (to be hot), the word *nonchalant,* describing someone who stays cool. Those of you who collect coincidences may wish to note that one of the most nonchalant movie characters in recent memory, played by Paul Newman, was known as Cool Hand Luke.

maggot

Q: In my practice as a musician playing music from the late Renaissance period, I sometimes come across tunes with titles like "Dick's Maggot" or "My Lady Winwood's Maggot." My dictionary gives as a definition for *maggot* "an extravagant notion, a whim," as well as the definition I am more familiar with, having to do with worms, putrefaction, and decay. Now my curiosity has been piqued. How did this word come to have these two so widely different meanings?

— *Steven S., via the Internet.*

Ah, you're one of those lute-and-flute guys, right? I used to work in an office with a fellow who moonlighted as a knight at one of those Renaissance fair deals. You know, the sort of outdoor dinner-theater costume pageants where your waiter wears tights and addresses you as *milord* or *milady?* Anyway, he didn't last long in our office, probably because he kept referring to the boss as *that fat varlet.*

Somehow I never thought I'd be writing a column about maggots, but here we go. The most common use of *maggot* is, as you note, to mean "a worm or grub," usually the larva of a fly. *Maggot,* which first appeared around 1398, is thought to have derived from the Middle English word *mathek,* which also meant "worm" and may have ultimately been Norse in origin.

The use of *maggot* in the name of musical pieces started in the early eighteenth century. The rather unlikely coupling of the name for a grub with a light tune meant for dancing is a little less bizarre when we note that, starting in the early seventeenth century, *maggot* was used figuratively to mean "a fanciful whim or silly idea." The logic behind this sense of *maggot* was, you guessed it, that crazy ideas were jokingly said to be the result of having maggots cavorting in one's cranium, the seventeenth-century equivalent of having bats in the belfry. Thus, a whimsical or "unserious" bit of music was jocularly christened "Dick's Maggot" or whatever.

Crazy ideas were jokingly said to be the result of having MAGGOTS cavorting in one's cranium.

Speaking of maggots, incidentally, one early form of the word was *mawk,* and *mawkish* originally meant "to be disgusted," as if by putrid meat. Only in the eighteenth century did *mawkish* come to mean "disgustingly oversentimental."

moxie

Q: If possible, could you help me with the origins of the word *moxie*? —*Tim M., via the Internet.*

Well, O.K., as long as I don't have to drink the stuff. Although many people know *moxie* only as a synonym for "gumption" or "courage," Moxie is and has been for over one hundred years a soft drink whose (inexplicable, in my opinion) popularity is confined largely to New England. The taste of Moxie is hard to describe, but if you have some really old sarsaparilla or birch beer around the house, mix it with a little battery acid and you'll get the general idea. My father, who grew up in Boston and claimed to actually like the stuff, kept a dozen or so bottles of Moxie on the back porch during my childhood. Whenever anyone would complain that there was no Coke or Pepsi in the house to drink, Pop would suggest we give Moxie another try. That Moxie lurking out there on the porch probably explains my lifelong fondness for tap water.

Anyone who has actually tasted Moxie will not be surprised to learn that it began life not as a soft drink but as a patent medicine. Invented by Dr. Augustin Thompson of Lowell, Massachusetts, in 1884, Moxie was originally marketed as *Moxie Nerve Food* and sold as a remedy for whatever might be ailing turn-of-the-century Americans. Moxie was enormously popular all over the United States, but in 1906 the passage of the Pure Food and Drug Act put an end to Moxie's medicinal claims, and from then on it was sold as a soft drink. It remained

Were You the Party That Ordered the Clean Glass?

f you happen to harbor the eminently reasonable conviction that computers have degraded the quality of everyday life, here's another bit of ammunition for your argument. The computerized ordering systems increasingly in use in many restaurants have probably sounded the death knell for diner or lunch-counter slang. Developed as a vocabulary of easily understood shorthand communication between waiters and short-order cooks, diner slang appeared along with the first lunch counters in the mid–nineteenth century. Once one of the most joyously creative examples of occupational jargon and the source of such enduring Americanisms as *BLT* (bacon, lettuce, and tomato sandwich), *sunnyside* (fried eggs with the yolks showing), *mayo* (mayonnaise), and *moo juice* (milk), diner slang has been disappearing ever since the first fast-food franchise sank its soulless roots into America's roadside.

Ironically, the one hope for survival of diner slang may rest with the wave of "fifties nostalgia" restaurants popping up across the United States, where teenage waiters are trained to shout "Wreck two, whiskey down" (see below) to the kitchen (while surreptitiously pushing the equivalent buttons on a computer, of course).

Here's a sampling of classic diner slang terms. Get 'em while they're hot.

MERRY CHRISTMAS

all the way: A sandwich with everything: lettuce, tomato, mayo, onion, and whatever else may seem appropriate to the cook.

B and B: A side order of bread and butter.

belch water: Seltzer.

Bossy in a bowl: Beef stew.

bowl of red: Chili.

breath: Onion.

burn the British: Toasted English muffin.

cackle-berries: Eggs.

Coney: Hot dog (also called a *dog, bun pup,* and *bow-wow*).

down: Toasted.

draw one: Cup of coffee.

FBI: Franks and beans.

java: Coffee (also *joe*).

merry Christmas: Tuna sandwich on toast with lettuce and tomato.

O.J.: Orange juice.

over: Eggs fried on both sides (also called *flopping,* (as in "Flop two!").

pistol: Pastrami.

put out the lights and cry: Liver and onions.

sinkers: Doughnuts.

stack: Pancakes.

sweep the kitchen: Hash (also known as *gentleman will take a chance*).

whiskey: Rye bread (a pun on *rye whiskey*).

with wings: An order to go (also *go for a walk* and *on wheels*).

wreck: Scramble (eggs).

MOXIE was originally marketed as *Moxie Nerve Food* and sold as a remedy for whatever might be ailing turn-of-the-century Americans.

popular, however, and with Moxie being Calvin Coolidge's favorite drink in the 1920s, the Moxie empire seemed secure. But Moxie's star began to wane as the kingdom of Coca-Cola slowly took over the market, and Moxie retreated to its New England home.

No one knows for sure why Dr. Thompson picked the name *Moxie* in the first place, but his promotion of the drink as a source of "pep and vigor" is, according to Moxie partisans, the source of its slang connotation of "courage." Personally, I think that anyone who takes a second sip of Moxie must have moxie to spare.

mufti

Q: I would be very grateful for any explanation regarding the origin of the word *mufti*. This is an expression commonly used to describe casual business dress code in the United Kingdom. I suspect this word may stem from British colonial rule in India, but I am unable to substantiate this theory.

—*Matthew M., via the Internet.*

Close, as we say in the United States, but no cigar, although it was a very good guess. This is the first time I've heard the word *mufti* applied to "casual day" in offices, probably because *mufti* is more commonly heard in the United Kingdom than in the United States. Not that U.S. workers are slouches when it comes to slouching, of course. I worked for many years in an office and took great pride in forging my own personal "casual day" all week long. I would just periodically declare, in the most ominous tone I could muster, "I'm very sorry, but I cannot wear a necktie. Neckties cause insanity," and my superiors would leave me alone.

Strictly speaking, *mufti* (pronounced "MUFF-tee") refers to civilian clothes worn by someone, such as a member of the military, who ordinarily wears a uniform. A soldier on leave, for instance, might well relish the chance to lounge around in mufti and not worry about polishing a lot of silly brass (either literally or metaphorically).

Mufti is indeed a relic of the British colonial experience, though its roots are in the Middle East, not India. A mufti is a Muslim judge, from the Arabic word meaning "to give a legal decision," the same word that gave us *fatwa* or *fetwa* (religious decree), brought to popular attention by the Iranian death sentence proclaimed against the author Salman Rushdie some years ago.

Just how an Arabic word for a Muslim jurist came to mean "casual dress" is a bit unclear.

Just how an Arabic word for a Muslim jurist came to mean "casual dress" is a bit unclear. But experts theorize that the first use of *mufti* in English was in

reference to the costumes used to portray Arab potentates in popular Western stage dramas in the nineteenth century. These getups
were highly exotic and colorful, making *mufti* a fitting metaphor
for a style of dress that was as unmilitary as possible.

nerd

Q: I am writing to you to inquire about the origin of
the word *nerd*. I have argued to many people my be-
lief that this word was originally coined on the 1970s TV series
Happy Days (by Fonzie). My opponents claim that this word
was actually in use in the 1950s (the setting of *Happy Days*).
Can you help with this?

— *Sean E., Marietta, Georgia, via the Internet.*

Say, you're not the guy who sent me the "Word Nerd"
T-shirt on my last birthday, are you? If so, you got the size
wrong—I wear a large, not a runt. I get no respect around here.

In any case, I do think I can cast some light on your debate
with your friends, although I'm not sure it's going to be helpful,
because I'm afraid they are right. The earliest recorded use of
the word *nerd* in print dates back to 1957, roughly the same
time as the setting of *Happy Days*. You're not entirely wrong,
however, since the term only gained widespread popularity in
the 1970s, almost certainly due to Fonzie's efforts.

I suppose we ought to take a moment here to define *nerd*
for the benefit of those readers who have never heard the word

(and, consequently, probably are pretty good working defini-
tions of *nerd* themselves). A nerd is a studious but socially
maladjusted person, almost always considered an outcast by
his or her peers. Common synonyms include *dork, dweeb, geek,*
and *loser,* although there are subtle differences among those
categories.

The origin of the word *nerd* is hazy; it may just
be a variation on the 1940s slang term *nert,* itself a
variant of *nut.* But one theory traces it to a surprising
source—Theodor Geisel, also known as Dr. Seuss.
In *If I Ran the Zoo* (1950), a Seuss character says,
"And then, just to show them, I'll sail to Ka-Troo /
And Bring Back . . . a Nerkle a Nerd and a Seer-
sucker, too!" Geisel invented his *nerd* as a nonsense
word with no apparent connection to nerds as we
know them today. Still, given the enormous popularity of the Seuss books, this may actually be the origin
of our modern *nerd.*

One theory
traces NERD to
a surprising
source—
Theodor Geisel,
also known as
Dr. Seuss.

newfangled

Q: Whilst reading through a brief dissertation on the
construction of windmills, I came across a drawing of
a device called a *fangle.* It was used for marking out the cogs
of the great gears. Clearly, I thought, this must be the source of
the word *newfangled.* On further thought, I wondered if *newfangled* would simply mean "new teeth cut for old gears," or

whether those resourceful millwrights were looking for improvements to their gadgets to cut such gears. What do the pundits think? —*Eric C., Calgary, Canada.*

I don't know what the pundits think, Eric. I had to get rid of them last week. Just the cost of pundit chow was bankrupting me, and their constant chattering was unbearable. And for all that trouble, not once did they use the word *whilst,* as you have, which earns you ten points right off the bat.

I'm not sure what to make of your discovery of a gear-making gizmo called a *fangle,* except that it is definitely not the source of our word *newfangled,* meaning "of a new kind." That honor goes to the Old English verb *fangol,* which meant "inclined to take." This word *fangol* is, as you might suspect, related to our modern *fang.* I guess if you've got fangs you're inclined to take, and most people are inclined to let you.

I guess if you've got fangs you're inclined to take, and most people are inclined to let you.

At some point *fangol* (by then *fangel* in Middle English) got hooked up with *newe* (new), giving us *newefangel,* with the composite meaning of "inclined toward or fond of new things." From there it was a short jump in the sixteenth century to the use of *newfangled* to describe the newness of the things themselves. *Newfangled* is, as I'm sure you know, always used in a derogatory sense, with the implication that the newfangled thing is silly or unnecessary.

Interestingly enough, once *newfangled* meant "of a brand-new kind," some people got a bit confused and decided that *fangle* was a separate word that must mean "silly gizmo" or "novelty." (This creation of a word that seems to be implied in a longer word is called *back formation* by linguists. *Sculpt,* for example, didn't exist until someone decided that it must be lurking within *sculpture.*) So there was actually a word *fangle* in English for a while, although it is largely obsolete today. But it is possible that this sense of *fangle* meaning "gizmo" was the reason they called the gear-making device you discovered a fangle.

Nosey Parker

Q: I have always wondered, but truthfully have never pursued, the origin of the saying "He/she is a Nosey Parker." I am particularly interested as my paternal grandmother was a Parker. If you can help me on this one, I thank you in advance. —*Patricia B., via the Internet.*

Now then, class, we can observe in this letter a particularly sophisticated example of the phenomenon known to devotees of psychobabble as *denial.* Ms. B. begins her letter with an admission that she has always wondered what a Nosey Parker might be but then hastens to assure us that she has never investigated the question. She then attempts to blame her all-consuming curiosity on her grandmother, hoping to deflect her audience from the growing realization that Ms. B. herself is, you guessed it, a Nosey Parker. Well, you can relax, Ms. B., you're among friends. Nobody here but us snoops.

Just how *Nosey Parker* came to mean "snoop" or "busy-body" is a mystery. Since the *Parker* is almost always capitalized, most popular theories interpret it as a proper name and go

looking for an especially inquisitive Parker in history. The leading candidate for the original Nosey Parker is Matthew Parker, archbishop of Canterbury from 1559 to 1575, who was evidently famous for his interest in other people's business.

The original NOSEY PARKERS were voyeurs who skulked about London's Hyde Park spying on amorous couples.

The problem with the archbishop theory, however, is that Nosey Parker only cropped up in written English in 1907, several centuries after Matthew Parker had stopped snooping around. A more likely explanation, outlined by Hugh Rawson in his marvelous book *Wicked Words,* is that the original Nosey Parkers were voyeurs who skulked about London's Hyde Park spying on amorous couples. Bolstering this theory is the fact that park keepers in England used to be known as *parkers,* and it strikes me that, in that preautomotive age, jokes involving nosey parkers were probably as common as our modern "cop on Lovers' Lane" variety was in the 1950s. And since *parker* most likely refers to an avocation and not a proper name, *nosey parker* need not be capitalized.

nutshell, in a

Q: Can you please tell me the origin of *in a nutshell?* You better hurry because I won't be online after September

26, because our company is going out of business . . . and that's
the whole truth in a nutshell!   — *Ska7, via the Internet.*

And thereby, as Shakespeare used to say, maybe hangs a
tale. I don't wish to appear to be picking on you in your hour of
unemployment, but I cannot but wonder whether your apparent penchant for noodling around on the Internet while supposedly working might not be intimately connected to your
impending disconnection. Are you sure that your company is
really going out of business, or is it possible that they're just
telling you that? My parents, for example, told me they were
moving to Istanbul while I was away at college back in 1970,
but I later discovered that they'd never even left the house. I'd
check on this if I were you
   In a nutshell, as I'm sure you know, means "in a few words"
or "very briefly explained." Nutshells, being the hard covering
enclosing the kernel of a nut, don't get very big, since
nuts themselves are generally fairly small. (There probably was a Jurassic walnut or something way back
when that could crunch Des Moines, but that screenplay is yet to be written.) Nutshells themselves were
first used as metaphors for something very small back
in 1602, when Shakespeare had Hamlet declare, "O
God, I could be bounded in a nutshell, and count myself a king of infinite space," whatever that meant.
Anything that could fit in a nutshell would have to be
pretty darn small, and by the eighteenth century all the
major writers were cramming things into nutshells.

By the
eighteenth
century all the
major writers
were cramming
things into
NUTSHELLS.

With a metaphor being as popular as *in a nutshell* has been, can the verb *to nutshell* (meaning "to briefly summarize") be far behind? Well, before we all start groaning about rampant verbification and the decline of our language, some news: *to nutshell* in this sense has been around since 1883, having first appeared in Mark Twain's *Life on the Mississippi*.

O.K.

Q: What is the origin of the abbreviation *O.K.*, meaning "all right"? — *Stephen D., via the Internet.*

I'm glad that you kept your question short, because the answer is pretty long.

H. L. Mencken once described *O.K.* as "the most successful of all Americanisms," an estimation verified during the Second World War by U.S. troops, who reported encountering the phrase all over the world. Of all the scores of theories (and subtheories) as to the origin of *O.K.*, the most widely heard traces *O.K.* to the O.K. Club, a political committee supporting Martin Van Buren's unsuccessful bid for reelection to the presidency in 1840. The *O.K.*, it is said, was short for *Old Kinderhook*, Van Buren's nickname (taken from his birthplace, the town of Kinderhook, New York).

It appears that this theory is not so much wrong (the O.K. Club certainly existed) as it is incomplete. Chances are good that Van Buren's partisans would never have named their club

O.K. had not *O.K.* and its variant spelling, *okay*, already been widely known as slang abbreviations of *oll korrect*, a humorous misspelling of *all correct*. American speech in the early nineteenth century was awash in similar abbreviations, two of which, *N.G.* (for *no good*) and *P.D.Q.* (for *pretty damn quick*), are still heard today. The serendipitous coincidence of Van Buren's nickname with one of the "hot" slang phrases of the day must have struck his political handlers as a great stroke of luck. Unfortunately, they quickly ran plumb out of luck, and Van Buren lost the election.

Ironically, while *O.K.* didn't save Van Buren's campaign, his campaign gave *O.K.* a new lease on life—until then, it had never been as popular as a competing phrase, *O.W.* (standing for *oll wright*). Without Martin Van Buren and his spin doctors, we might be saying *O.W.* to this day.

H. L. Mencken once described O.K. as "the most successful of all Americanisms."

paddy wagon

Q: Last Sunday afternoon, I heard a discussion on a radio talk show about the use of the term *paddy wagon*. The host insisted that the term is a terrible slam against the Irish. He likened it to using *wop* against an Italian. A caller, who was Irish, disagreed, saying that the term *paddy* came about because of the nickname for policemen, which referred to St. Patrick, and *wagon* just meant the vehicle they used to pick up the people who were creating a disturbance. Can you shed any enlightenment? —*Jo K., via the Internet.*

Certainly. I shed enlightenment the way my cat sheds fur—in great orange clumps. I've never figured out, since we're on the subject (involuntarily, in your case), how cat fur ends up inside the microwave. Does he make popcorn the minute I leave the house? Is he whipping up dinner for all his pals while I'm gone? Is that where all the instant mashed potatoes went?

As far as your question goes, you have already heard the two likely answers, and no one knows which is the truth. The use of *paddy wagon* as a slang term for a police van dates back to the 1920s and seems to have originated in either Philadelphia or New York City, cities that had both large Irish immigrant populations and largely Irish American police forces during that period.

It is true that *Paddy,* a familiar form of the common Irish name *Padraic* (or *Patrick*), was used in the nineteenth and early twentieth centuries as a generic, and often uncomplimentary, term for an Irishman, both in the United States and England. But while *paddy* certainly was used as an insult in the past, and the Irish were without doubt the victims of discrimination, I think that it takes a pretty thin skin to find a grave insult in the term *paddy wagon.* Among other things, the fact that it remains unclear whether *paddy* referred to the arresting officer or the miscreant being arrested rather clouds the logic of taking offense. That *paddy* is also

The use of PADDY WAGON as a slang term for a police van dates back to the 1920s.

EVAN MORRIS

used in nonpejorative senses (*Saint Paddy's Day*) has also robbed the word of its sting, as opposed to words such as *wop,* which have always been, and probably always will be, grave insults.

pandemonium

Q: My husband and I disagree as to the origin of the word *pandemonium.* I say the word was formed early in the twentieth century when pandas were brought to the United States and caused much curiosity. My husband says the word stems from *Pandora's box,* meaning "a source of confusion." Who's right, or is neither one of us right?

—*Barbara B., via the Internet.*

First of all, thanks for a great question. You folks have come up with two marvelously inventive theories. Unfortunately, they are also both wrong. But I really like the one about pandas.

Your husband's hunch about *Pandora's box* is a good one. As I'm sure we all recall (cough, cough), the Greek myth of Pandora recounts the story of a very curious woman who could not resist the temptation to open a mysterious forbidden box. Too late, Pandora discovered that in opening the box she had set free all the evils—War, Sickness, Poverty, etc.— that plague the world today. Confusion must have

The word **PANDEMONIUM** was coined by the poet John Milton in his epic poem *Paradise Lost.*

been somewhere in that box, too, but we can't pin pandemonium on poor Pandora.

The word *pandemonium,* meaning "mass disorder and chaos," was coined by the poet John Milton in his epic poem *Paradise Lost* in 1667. Milton invented the word as a name for the capital of Hell in his poem, the place where Satan held gatherings of all his underlings and minions. Milton himself spelled the word *pandaemonium* and concocted it by combining the Greek *pan* (all) with the Latin *daemonium* (demon). *Pandaemonium* is still considered an acceptable alternate spelling today.

Although Milton had created *pandemonium* as the name of a specific locale, by the nineteenth century the word was being used as a synonym for any center of vice or depravity. The term was broadened still further in the twentieth century, as *pandemonium* has come to mean "an uproar" or "an extremely disorderly situation."

peacoat

Q: Where did the term *peacoat* come from? I know what a peacoat is, but I would like to know the origin of its name. —*Paige, via the Internet.*

Ah, pea jackets. I had a dandy pea jacket many years ago. It was during my Russian Intellectual phase, when I would stalk the streets glowering at small children, attired in a thick black turtleneck sweater, my trusty pea jacket, and the heaviest volume of Dostoevsky I could rustle up in central Ohio. Anyone who has experienced August in Ohio will understand why I dumped that getup fairly quickly.

Pea jackets, as any old salt knows, are the hip-length, double-breasted, dark blue cold-weather coats issued to sailors. Made from heavy wool, pea jackets have been standard naval issue since at least the eighteenth century and are still worn by the sailors of many countries today, including U.S. Navy personnel below the grade of chief petty officer.

Any item that has been around as long as the pea jacket is bound to generate a variety of legends about its origins, and pea jackets have spawned at least two. The most colorful, so to speak, traces the *pea* to the tendency of neophyte sailors, not yet accustomed to the rolling seas, to turn pea green from seasickness. The charm of this theory is the image it conjures of a young sailor asking why his newly issued coat is called a *pea jacket* and receiving that quite possibly self-fulfilling prophecy as an answer.

A more sober theory decodes *pea jacket* as originally being *p-jacket,* with the *p* standing for *pilot,* the person who steers a ship into and out of a harbor. While this theory is not impossible, it turns out to be unnecessary: the *pea* in *pea jacket* almost certainly comes from the obsolete English word *pee,* which meant "a coat made of coarse cloth." *Pee* in turn probably came from the Dutch word *pie* (*pij* in modern Dutch), found in the term *pijjakker,* meaning a coat very similar to our modern pea jacket.

PEA JACKETS
are still worn
by U.S. Navy
personnel below
the grade of
chief petty
officer.

Pecksniffian

Q: A recent article in the *New York Times* characterized Philadelphia as Pecksniffian. Is this a Dickensian reference? What does it mean? —*Jacque B., via the Internet.*

It means that the *Times* had better hope that it doesn't run into Philadelphia in a dark alley, that's what it means. You'll notice that those *Times* guys don't dare talk that way about Chicago or Detroit. They know they'd be sleeping with the fishes in a New York minute if they did. I guess Philadelphia, with all that brotherly love stuff, comes across as Wimp City. Still, the *Times* had better watch its back. I've seen how they drive in Philadelphia. Life is cheap there.

The Third Law states that if any reader asks about a Dickensian reference, it will inevitably be a reference to a Dickens novel the columnist never quite got around to reading.

Pecksniffian is indeed a Dickensian reference, which is to say that it refers to a character in one of Charles Dickens's novels, in this case *Martin Chuzzlewit*, published in 1844. This seems as good a moment as any to explain the dreaded Third Law of Column Writing. The Third Law states that if any reader asks about a Dickensian reference, it will inevitably be a reference to a Dickens novel the columnist never quite got around to reading. That's right, mea culpa, I've never read *Martin Chuzzlewit*. I did, however, read *David Copperfield* twice, which ought to count for something.

In any case, it seems that Dickens's Mr. Pecksniff

was an insufferable hypocrite, always propounding a philosophy of moral rectitude and benevolence while actually being a greedy, duplicitous creep. Part of Dickens's genius was to populate his novels with characters that embodied and epitomized classic human foibles and failings. Since nearly all of Dickens's readers had already encountered at least one Mr. Pecksniff in their daily lives, the term *Pecksniff* almost instantly became common shorthand for a pious hypocrite.

Just how all this could possibly apply to the City of Brotherly Love is a bit of a mystery, though I suppose the *Times* means to imply that it is actually the City of Pious Hypocrites. No wonder Philadelphia is ticked off.

pedigree

Q: Can you tell me the origin of *pedigree?* My uncle says that it comes from farmers examining the feet of horses to judge their parentage.   —*D. O., Columbus, Ohio.*

You might ask your uncle if he happens to know the origin of *malarkey,* meaning "nonsense." Actually, to be fair, he has a foot in the door to the real origin of *pedigree,* as there is indeed a foot involved. *Pedigree,* meaning "ancestry" or "lineage," comes from the Old French phrase *pie de grue,* which translates as "crane's foot." What could a large bird's foot possibly have to do with anyone's ancestry? Well, when genealogists draw a chart to illustrate a family tree, offspring are shown as descending from their parents by means of forked lines that look like, you guessed it, the spindly foot of a crane. Over the years, *pedigree,* which originally meant a way of showing ancestry, came to be a synonym for ancestry itself.

Returning to the question of judging horses for a moment, I think your uncle may have been thinking of a different part of the horse. A wise horse trader used to look in a horse's mouth before striking a bargain, because a horse's age (if not its lineage) can be determined by the amount of wear on its teeth. Naturally, if the horse was a gift, only the most ungrateful recipient would think to check its teeth before accepting, thus the adage "Don't look a gift horse in the mouth."

What could a large bird's foot possibly have to do with anyone's ancestry?

Finally, rather than leave your uncle hanging, I must tell you that the origin of *malarkey* is a mystery. It sounds either Irish or Cockney to me, but we may never know for sure, which just proves that some of our best words come to us without pedigrees.

pickled as an owl

Q: In the Big Book of Alcoholics Anonymous the phrase *pickled as an owl* is used to describe a man who thought he could stay sober, but the next thing he knew, he was "*pickled as an owl.*" We know that it means he got drunk, but we can't find anyone who knows the origins of this saying. We always thought owls were much too smart to get intoxicated. Could you help us out on where in the heck this saying came from?

—*Rusty A., via the Internet.*

I'll give it a shot. Speaking of owls (and possibly of alcohol as well), I read a news item a while back about two men in England, neighbors who, in the course of conversation one day, discovered they had a common habit. Every evening, each would step out into his backyard and exchange hoots with a unseen nearby owl. I'll bet their wives knew all along that they were hooting at each other.

There are really two parts to your question. First is the use of *pickled* as a synonym for "drunk," one of the oldest of such similes, dating back to the early seventeenth century. But when I say "such similes," keep in mind that there are literally hundreds of synonyms for drunkenness, over 350 of which are listed in an appendix to the *Dictionary of American Slang* by Harold Wentworth and Stuart Berg Flexner. *Bent, blind, breezy, canned, cuckooed, fish-eyed, flooey, fuzzled, lathered, piped, pruned,* and *swozzled* are only a small sample. *Pickled,* to the extent that logic plays a role in these terms at all, was probably based on the image of a drunk being marinated or preserved in alcohol.

As to why an owl, the only possible answer is, why not? Nearly every other animal short of penguins has been maligned in this fashion. *Drunk as a* has been followed by, at various times, *pig, fly, fowl, lion, fish,*

Drunk as a has been followed by, at various times, pig, fly, fowl, lion, fish, loon, rat, tick, mouse, newt, and, of course, skunk.

Some Dunce in a Ritzy Cardigan Ate My Graham Cracker

What's in a name? Well, if you play your cards right (or spectacularly wrong), your very own personal name might end up immortalized as a common English word, spoken every day by people who probably won't have the vaguest idea that they're talking about you. Being enshrined in a word might not be the kind of immortality many of us would prefer (as Woody Allen put it, "I don't want to achieve immortality through my work . . . I want to achieve it through not dying"), but it beats the heck out of carving your name in the nearest tree.

English is full of words and phrases coined from the names of people (or groups or places), called *eponyms,* from the Greek *epi* (upon) and *onyma* (name). Some eponyms are easily recognized as such. But the most successful eponyms are arguably the ones that have entered English so smoothly that we don't even recognize them as anything other than simple words. Here are a few examples of these everyday eponyms:

cardigan: The collarless buttoned sweater made famous by Ozzie Nelson in the old TV series *The Adventures of Ozzie and Harriet* and now commonly worn by actors portraying college professors. Named after James Thomas Brudenell, the corrupt and incompetent seventh earl of Cardigan, who supposedly wore a similar garment while commanding his troops in the Crimean War. The earl is primarily remembered for leading the disastrous charge of the Light Brigade at Balaklava, which the earl conveniently survived, while most of his hapless men ("Theirs not to reason why,/ Theirs but to do and die," in the words of Tennyson's poem) did not.

chauvinism: Superpatriotism of the fanatically mindless sort, lately expanded to include blind loyalty to or a blinkered view of any group or issue (as in "male chauvinism"). Named for Nicolas Chauvin, a French soldier wounded seventeen times while serving under Napoleon. Retired with honors, Chauvin returned to his village and immediately set about boring the ears off his neighbors with impassioned, irrational, and incessant tributes to the infallibility of his idol Napoleon, even after the emperor's defeat at Waterloo and subsequent exile.

dunce: A dull-witted, stupid person, incapable of learning and often portrayed in old cartoons as a child sitting in a classroom corner wearing a conical dunce cap. Based, in one of history's most unfair turnabouts, on the name of John Duns Scotus (ca. 1266–1308), among the most celebrated of medieval philosophers. Though Duns Scotus was a brilliant and subtle theologian (known as *Doctor subtilis,* Latin for "the Subtle Doctor," in fact), his followers in the following centuries (known as the *Dunsmen*) were so closed-minded and pigheadedly resistant to change that they became known as first *dunses,* then *dunces.*

graham cracker: A semisweet cracker made with whole wheat flour. Invented by and named for Sylvester Graham (1794–1851), a Presbyterian minister who became convinced that eating meat caused lewd behavior and that ketchup caused insanity. Graham embarked on a crusade to convince America to eat pure foods, exercise, spend more time outdoors, and especially to abstain from white bread. Graham crackers, believe it or not, were one weapon in his arsenal. Graham had tens of thousands of followers in the early nineteenth century and was probably right about many things, although he was definitely wrong about ketchup.

ritzy: Ostentatiously fancy or lavish; pretentiously haughty. From the name of César Ritz (1850–1918), Swiss-born hotelier famous for his high-class hotels in Paris, London, and New York. High quality, exceptional service, and obsessive attention to detail made the Ritz hotels a magnet for the wealthy and famous and enshrined the name Ritz as the gold standard of luxury. Checkout time, however, was still noon.

loon, rat, tick, mouse, newt, and, of course, *skunk.* Again, logic does not loom large in such imagery, but the choice of an owl may have been in reference to the perceived similarity of an owl's wide gaze to a drunk's glassy stare.

pig in a poke

Q: Can you please tell me what the phrase *pig in a poke* is supposed to mean? My mother has used it my whole life, and she doesn't even know what it means.

—*Lisa B., via the Internet.*

Well, your mother must have some idea what *pig in a poke* means, mustn't she? After all, she doesn't use it as an all-purpose expression of amazement ("Pig in a poke! That's a good cup of coffee!") or, conversely, as a scathing epithet ("That Muriel, she's a real little pig in a poke"). My guess is that she knows that *to buy a pig in a poke* means "to buy something without seeing it or being certain of its value." Your mother just doesn't know what a poke is or what a pig would be doing in one.

That's not surprising, given how rarely one sees a poke these days. The *poke* in *pig in a poke* is an archaic word for "bag" or "sack." When you went to market hundreds of years ago, you'd most likely come home with your purchases in such a poke—not one of those filmy and annoying things you get at supermarkets today, but a proper sack, made of burlap or canvas or the like.

Since merchants at the farmers' markets of fourteenth-century Europe varied in their honesty, a smart shopper would be careful to check the poke he was handed to be sure that it really contained what he had paid for. This was especially important in the case of big-ticket purchases, such as a live suckling pig, since unscrupulous merchants were not above substituting a stray cat of the appropriate weight for the pig in the poke handed to an unwary purchaser. The phrase *don't buy a pig in a poke,* originally practical advice for fourteenth-century shoppers, eventually came to be a warning applicable to any situation in which we are asked to accept an unfamiliar object or idea on faith.

Your mother just doesn't know what a poke is or what a pig would be doing in one.

By the way, can you guess what other common phrase came from the moment when the dishonest merchant's ruse was revealed and the buyer learned the true nature of his purchase? That's right—*letting the cat out of the bag.*

polka dot

Q: Do you know the origin of *polka dot?* A friend has been wondering for years about this, and I would like to give him an answer. —*B. K., via the Internet.*

You're never going to believe this, but I've actually been waiting years to answer your friend's question. Honest. Every morning I trudge out past the cows to the mailbox, murmuring

A variety of
manufacturers
cashed in on
the public's
POLKA mania
by naming a
dizzying range
of products
after the dance.

"Polka dot, polka dot" to myself in a hopeful mantra. But day after day I find the well dry, polka-dot–wise, and must face the long walk back past those smirking cows. Night falls, and I sit glumly in the corner at parties while my friends nudge each other and whisper, "Ask him about the goldarn polka dots, Bernice. I can't take any more of this." But it's not the same as a real reader question.

So now, at long last, the polka dot saga. Back in the mid–nineteenth century, the United States was awash in polka dots, that pattern of dots of uniform size and arrangement, because we had all gone polka crazy. The polka, of course, is a simple, lively dance step that took Europe and America by storm soon after its introduction in 1835. The name *polka* is a minor mystery. Although *polka* is Polish for "Polish woman," the polka dance is actually of Bohemian origin, and *polka* may be a corruption of the Czech word *pulka* (half), referring to the short half steps involved in the dance.

None of which, I realize, explains polka dots, but I'm getting to that. At the peak of the polka craze, from about 1840 to 1890 (this was a very long craze), a variety of manufacturers cashed in on the public's polka mania by naming a dizzying range of products after the dance. Polka hats, polka gauze, polka curtain ties, and, of course, polka-dot fabrics had little or nothing to do with the dance but sold like hotcakes, for a few years anyway. The polka-dot pattern, however, had staying power and remains popular today, especially in neckties.

pony up

Q : Do you know the origin of the phrase *pony up* (meaning "to pay an account or fine")? How about *pony keg*, the name for a small keg of beer?

—Al H., via the Internet.

Well, I have a pony question of my own: where the heck is my pony? Every year since I was about five years old I have asked for a pony as a birthday gift. Now, several decades (ahem) later, I have yet to get my pony. Please don't give me any guff about a fourth-floor apartment in Manhattan not being a suitable home for a pony. If ponies can make it up those mountains in Scotland, a few flights of stairs should be no problem, and I promise not to take my pony on the subway. As you can see, I have been quite patient, but enough's enough. Pony up the pony.

The nice thing about your question is that both the uses of *pony* you ask about come from the basic sense of *pony* as "a small horse." A pony, strictly speaking, is a small breed of horse, rather than simply a young horse, which is called a *foal.* The root of *pony* was the Latin *pullus,* meaning any young animal (which is still with us in the form *pullet,* meaning "a young chicken"). *Pullus* became the Old French *poulain* (foal), whence came the diminutive *poulenet,* which then trotted over to Scotland and showed up as *powney,* which was later anglicized to *pony.*

A PONY,
strictly
speaking, is
a small breed
of horse, rather
than simply a
young horse.

To *pony up* and *pony keg* both embody the "smallness" aspect of *pony*. *Pony* has meant "a small amount of money" since the late eighteenth century, when it specifically meant "the sum of twenty-five pounds sterling" (which was actually a hefty hunk of change at the time, but go figure). To *pony up* thus meant "to settle a small debt." *Pony kegs* are smaller than standard tavern-sized kegs, by analogy to a *pony* of liquor, which has meant "a small glass of spirits" since the mid–nineteenth century.

pork barrel

Q: News about our government on any given day usually has at least one story about what is called *pork-barreling* or just *pork*. Despite everyone's desire to reduce or eliminate it, it still continues and probably will be a fixture among our legislators forevermore. I know that it refers to patronage appointments by politicians, or the procuring of lucrative contracts for their home districts, but I'm confounded as to the origin of this term. I don't even know what a *pork barrel* is! Any suggestions, since my previously trusty *Webster's Ninth* has let me down?

—*Tae, via the Internet.*

Apropos of pork, your question leads me to wonder how the movie *Babe*, recipient of so many accolades a few years ago, has affected pork consumption in this country. I can just imagine how the pork industry, which has spent the last few years strenuously touting pork as "the other white meat," feels about a hit movie starring a cute pig. Most children would probably sooner eat Lassie chops or roasted Muppets than pork at this point.

Pork barrel means, or meant, just what it sounds like—"a barrel full of pork," commonly found in rural American kitchens in the nineteenth century. While a barrel of meat may seem a dubious food-storage choice to us today, back then the amount of pork to be found in a family's barrel was considered a reliable index of their prosperity. James Fenimore Cooper, writing in 1845, noted that "I hold a family to be in a desperate way, when the mother can see the bottom of the pork barrel."

Pork, in fact, played so central a role in nineteenth-century rural life that the word was generally used as a synonym for wealth, and, in particular, wealth derived from political graft and corruption. It wasn't that great a leap, therefore, to apply the image of a pork barrel to legislation aimed at benefiting a politician's own constituents (in effect filling their "pork barrels") and thus ensuring his reelection.

In the nineteenth century, the amount of PORK
to be found in a family's BARREL was considered
a reliable index of their prosperity.

posh

Q: I just found you on the Internet and was so surprised to learn that *posh* is not an acronym for *port outbound, starboard home*. As someone who wrote training programs and trained tour guides in Long Beach, California, I personally, or through the trainers, advised hundreds of tour guides on the Royal Mail Ship that that was exactly what *posh* meant. I'm pretty horrified by the number of people with wrong information for which I am responsible. Please advise me where the word does come from, and perhaps someone I trained will read your answer. Thanks!

—Debby M., via the Internet.

Aha! So you're the one! The fiendish Moriarty of Misinformation who has dogged my steps, lo these many years. The evil genius whose spurious *posh* stories have befuddled millions of innocent tourists. Quick, Watson, the net! We mustn't let her escape!

Just kidding. I know you're really just another innocent victim of the insidious *posh* thought virus. So here is the skinny on *posh*. The story you've heard (and retold) is that *posh* comes from the days of ocean travel between England and India. The wealthy, it was said, would be given the most desirable accommodations, which on that voyage boiled down to cabins on whichever side of the ship remained untouched by the blistering tropical sun. Such preferred arrangements were said to be *port* (left side) *out, starboard* (right side) *home,* neatly summed up in the acronym *P.O.S.H.,* which was stamped on the rich folks' tickets. The acronym *P.O.S.H.* then later became a synonym for "the best of everything."

You're really just another innocent victim of the insidious POSH thought virus.

It's a lovely theory—too bad there's not a shred of evidence in its favor, and a good deal of evidence against it. Among other things, it seems that neither the crews of the ships in service on that route nor the owners of the steamship lines, when questioned about the term, had ever heard of it.

The truth? *Posh* is an actual word in Romany, the language of the Gypsies, meaning "half." *Posh* originally entered the argot of England's underworld in the seventeenth century in such compounds as *posh-houri,* meaning "halfpence," and soon became a slang term for "money" in general. From there it was a short hop to meaning "expensive" or "fancy." Voilà, *posh.*

pot, going to

Q: On a recent trip to Turkey we were visiting an ancient ruin where people were buried in large pots. When the next family member died, we were told, he or she would be put in the same pot. Does this have any relation to our expression *going to pot?*

—*Edie, via the Internet.*

I knew there was a reason why I never visited Turkey. But, of course, I mustn't presume to judge the burial traditions of another culture. After all, my own youth was spent tending to an informal pet cemetery in our suburban backyard, where row after row of goldfish, turtles, hamsters, and the occasional unlucky sparrow were interred with all due solemnity. To this day I cannot bring myself to throw away shoe boxes and similar small containers, although I do keep them in the basement so as not to unnecessarily discomfit the current menagerie.

All my little clients had "gone to pot" in the figurative sense, meaning they had deteriorated or been destroyed, but I would never have dreamed of them "going to pot" in the original sense of the term. In 1542, when the phrase first appeared, *to go to pot* meant "to be cut up like chunks of meat destined for the stew pot." Such a stew was usually the last stop for the remnants of a once-substantial cut of meat or poultry, so *going to pot* made perfect sense as a metaphor for anything, from a national economy to a marriage, that had seen better days. Early uses of the metaphor were usually in the form *go to the pot.*

In 1542, when the phrase first appeared, TO GO TO POT meant "to be cut up like chunks of meat destined for the stew pot."

Speaking of stew, it's a tribute to the enduring popularity of this combination of boiled vegetables and meat that almost every culture in the world has developed its own local version, from Hungarian goulash to Scottish hotchpotch (whence our *hodgepodge,* meaning "jumbled mixture"). We also still speak of someone slowly boiling with anger as being *in a stew,* and, if we decide to ignore him, he *stews in his own juices.*

EVAN MORRIS

potboiler

Q : Recently my father used the word *potboiler* to refer to a type of book. I wasn't familiar with the term, and he described it to me as light fiction, often a mystery. He supposed the term developed to mean something one would read to kill time, such as in waiting for a pot to boil. What's your view?

—*Laura V., via the Internet.*

Good question. To be honest, until I received your query, I had never given much thought to *potboiler*, though I have always, like your father, understood it to mean a kind of vaguely trashy novel of the sort often called *airport fiction*.

Your father's theory about a potboiler being something one reads while waiting for a pot to boil makes perfect sense. While I have not, personally, boiled many things in pots since the onset of the current eye-of-newt shortage, I have spent three or four years of my life in Laundromats waiting for an available dryer, so I know how low one's standards of literature can fall under such circumstances.

Samuel Johnson put it best: "No man but a blockhead ever wrote except for money."

As it turns out, this theory is slightly off base. A *potboiler* is, as the *Oxford English Dictionary* puts it, "a work of literature or art executed for the purpose of 'boiling the pot,' i.e., of gaining a livelihood." In other words, potboilers are created "strictly from hunger," as we say in the writing biz, as moneymakers rather than as works of art.

Potboiler has been used in this sense since around 1864, although writers have certainly been writing with food and shelter in mind pretty much ever since paper was invented. Perhaps it was the father of modern lexicography himself, Samuel Johnson, who put it best: "No man but a blockhead ever wrote except for money."

p's and q's

Q: My daughter asked me what *p's and q's* stands for in the phrase *mind your p's and q's* recently. I think it stands for *problems and questions,* but can't be sure.

—*Danielle, via the Internet.*

You are not alone. Folks have been saying *mind your p's and q's,* meaning "be very careful" or "behave yourself," since the late eighteenth century. There are a number of fascinating theories as to where the phrase came from, so you can pretty much take your pick of the following.

One theory is that the phrase comes from the practice in certain British pubs of tallying a customer's purchases on a blackboard behind the bar, with the notation *p* standing for *pints* and *q* for *quarts.* If a customer failed to pay close attention and mind his p's and q's, he might well find by evening's end that the barkeep had padded his tab.

Another theory, drawn from the schoolroom, is that any child approaching the mystery of penmanship soon discovers that the lowercase script *p* is devilishly easy to confuse with the lowercase *q*. Thus, the theory goes, generations of teachers exhorting their small charges to mind their p's and q's created an enduring metaphor for being attentive and careful. A different but similar theory centers on typesetters in old-fashioned type shops, where the danger of confusing lowercase *p* and *q* was increased because typesetters had to view the letters backwards.

Still other theories tie the *p* to *pea cloth* (the rough fabric used in pea jackets) and the *q* to *queue,* which meant "a ponytail," either that of the fancy wigs worn by courtiers of the day or the real ponytails commonly worn by sailors. In the upscale version of this theory, young aristocrats were cautioned not to get the powder from their wigs on their jackets made of pea cloth. The sailor version has old salts advising newcomers to dip their ponytails in tar (a common practice, believe it or not) but to avoid soiling their pea jackets with the tar.

Personally, I tend to lean toward the schoolroom theory, simply because it is so easy to imagine a teacher, faced with a class of rowdy children, advising them that their time would be better spent in perfecting their penmanship by minding their p's and q's than in roughhousing.

Any child approaching the mystery of penmanship
soon discovers that the lowercase script P is devilishly
easy to confuse with the lowercase Q.

quack

Q: I've been searching for the origins of using *quack* to describe a doctor or person to no avail. Can you help me? — *Carrie, via the Internet.*

A doctor or person, eh? That's an interesting distinction to draw. I think you may be hearing shortly from the American Medical Association about that one. Of course, when they finish with you, you'll still have quite a few offended waterfowl to answer to. I'm told that there's nothing that gets a duck's dander up faster than being used as a metaphor for a medical charlatan.

To begin at the beginning, *quack* has been used for the sound a duck makes since the sixteenth century. *Quack* is what linguists call an *echoic* or *imitative* word—it arose simply because folks thought it was a good approximation of the actual sound it describes.

I'm told that there's nothing that gets a duck's dander up faster than being used as a metaphor for a medical charlatan.

At about the same time that people decided that ducks quack, they also began to use *quack* to describe the sound made by itinerant patent-medicine salesmen made as they hawked their wares. These charlatans, who boasted endlessly about the miraculous properties of the ointments and potions they sold, were known as *quacksalvers*—they "quacked" about their "salves." The term *quacksalver* was quickly shortened in common usage, giving us *quack*.

Of course, back in the sixteenth and seventeenth centuries, medical science was in its infancy, and the field was awash in fakers and charlatans of all stripes. The term *quack* was fairly quickly expanded to include fraudulent "doctors" who advertised their ability to cure a wide variety of ailments but excelled only in relieving their patients of their wallets.

This use of *quack* to describe an unscrupulous or unqualified physician has been in constant use for more than three hundred years, probably because there is no lack of quacks even today. An accurate map of the modern medical world would still mark large regions with the warning *Here be quacks.*

raining cats and dogs

Q: It was a dark, windy night with clouds scudding across the sky. . . . It began to rain . . . and rain . . . and *rain cats and dogs.* From where does this phrase come? I've read about rains of frogs and toads and trees and other things. I was told that in one country things were so gloomy (rebellions and bad weather), it was reigning kings and queens.

—*Hicks, via the Internet.*

O.K., lad, let's be movin' along. There'll be none of that creative writing stuff on my beat. Next you'll be telling us that the road was a ribbon of silver in the moonlight and all that florid folderol. Then you and your beatnik buddies will be setting up a writing school, never mentioning to your poor students that becoming a writer means never getting to go outside again. Scribble, scribble, scribble, until your friends and family forget what you look like.

On the other hand, we do get to work in our pajamas. Now, as to cats and dogs, we're going to rely a little on another writer, Christine Ammer, who has produced a book called, fortuitously, *It's Raining Cats and Dogs — and Other Beastly Expressions.* The first verified use of *raining cats and dogs* was in 1738 by Jonathan Swift (of *Gulliver's Travels* fame), though there were earlier phrases that employed *cats* and/or *dogs* as metaphors for heavy rain.

Why would *cats and dogs* be a metaphor for a heavy downpour? According to Ms. Ammer, it may have been because in Northern European myths the cat stood for rain and the dog for wind. Or perhaps the clamor of a full-tilt thunderstorm reminded someone of the sound of cats and dogs fighting.

It's also possible that the phrase is a grisly reference to the fact that, as Ms. Ammer puts it, "In 17th century Britain, after a cloudburst the gutters would overflow with a filthy torrent that included dead animals. . . ." That's a bit too grim for my taste, so I'm going to stick with the bit about cats and dogs symbolizing wind and rain. As any good writing teacher will tell you, the first step in creative writing is always to edit reality.

In Northern European myths, the CAT stood for rain and the DOG for wind.

EVAN MORRIS

sabotage

Q: I had heard that the word *sabotage* had a meaning in French manufacturing history similar to what the term *Luddite* has in English manufacturing history, but I cannot confirm this. Can you help? — *Clarinat87, via the Internet.*

To answer your question, you and I will have to back up a bit, in case other readers don't know the story of *Luddite,* to which you refer.

According to legend, Ned Lud (or Ludd—opinions vary) was the "village idiot" of a town in Leicestershire, England, in 1779. One fine day, our boy Ned went completely bananas, ran into the shop of a textile manufacturer, and destroyed several of his looms for no good reason. This caused, as one might imagine, quite a stir at the time.

Now fast-forward a few years to about 1811, when English textile workers, their employment threatened by new mechanical looms, rebelled and started destroying the new machinery. Needing a catchy name, the rebels called themselves *Luddites* after old Ned, and ever since, the term has been applied to anyone who resists new technology.

Who wouldn't like to throw an occasional shoe (or wrench) into the machines that set our frenetic social pace?

The story you've probably heard about *sabotage* follows the same general outlines. *Sabot* is the French word for "a wooden shoe or clog." Various stories tell of French workers, like their English brethren, rebelling against the depredations of the Industrial Revolution, in this case by tossing their sabots into the newfangled machinery, bringing production to a halt.

It's an appealing story. After all, who wouldn't like to throw an occasional shoe (or wrench) into the machines that set our frenetic social pace? But there's no evidence that any sabots were ever tossed. *Sabotage* actually comes from the French verb *saboter,* which means "to make a loud clattering with wooden shoes." Metaphorically, the French use *sabotage* to mean "a botched musical performance," "any kind of bad job," or "the deliberate destruction of tools or machinery." This last meaning was the one carried over into English, where *sabotage* took on the additional meaning of "damage done clandestinely to impair an enemy's ability to fight."

salad days

Q: I've often heard the term *salad days* but never truly understood what was meant by it and certainly never knew the origin of the phrase. I've seen it used to refer to the early, less prosperous phase of a successful person's career. At least I think this is what they are implying. Can you help?

—*Mary S., Chicago, Illinois.*

I'll sure try, though I'm not much of a salad eater myself. It's not that I haven't tried, you understand. A few years ago I ac-

Shakespeare coined the term in his play
Antony and Cleopatra.

tually became a genuine full-throttle vegetarian, eschewing all meat, even chicken and fish. Too late I realized the grim truth: I loathe 99 percent of the vegetables on this planet. Subsisting on a diet consisting almost entirely of grilled cheese sandwiches, I was well on my way to turning a deep shade of yellow #5, when one night I had a remarkable dream. A chicken and a fish appeared before me and begged me to abandon my silly qualms and chow down on their tasty brethren. Never one to spurn spectral advice, I redefined *vegetable* first thing the next morning, and I am now right as rain.

You're almost right about the meaning of *salad days,* a term I haven't heard in quite a few years and one that I fear is fading from our language. A person's salad days are the days of youth, when he or she is "green" (without experience), but fresh and hopeful. Such a period is indeed likely to be less prosperous than the later years of a wealthy person, but I suppose someone who never makes any great amount of money could have had salad days as well. The important thing is the sense of crisp, fresh youth. And if that equation of youth with salad greens strikes you as a little corny, you'll have to take it up with Shakespeare, who coined the term *salad days* in his play *Antony and Cleopatra.*

Cat Got Your Tongue?

Pity the poor house cat. Her relatives, the lion, tiger, cheetah, puma, and leopard, are among the most feared and respected of creatures, legendary hunters celebrated throughout human history for their grace, speed, and ferocity. Our modern Miss Fur Ball, however, has been reduced to a pedestrian existence, cooling her heels on the couch waiting for someone to open a can of Fancy Feast and boring the dog with endless tales of how the ancient Egyptians considered her a god. Sic transit gloria Lion King.

On the other hand (the one covered with cat scratches in response to the preceding paragraph), *Felis catus* has exerted a profound influence on the English language. And with a few exceptions (*more than one way to skin a cat,* for example), our feline figures of speech are, if not always positive, nonetheless tributes to the common cat's agility, wiliness, independence, and perseverance. Here are a few examples.

cat burglar: Since about 1907, a burglar who enters silently and stealthily, gliding like a cat. A similar tribute to a cat's gracefulness, *to cat-foot,* or "walk as silently as a cat," has been in use since about 1916.

caterwaul: Since the time of Chaucer (1386), to screech and howl like cats fighting or a cat in heat. From Dutch and German roots meaning "cat wailing." A similar term, *katzenjammer,* from the German *katzen* (cats) and *jammer* (wailing), is used in English to mean a "hangover" or "a loud and raucous disturbance." Hans and Fritz Katzenjammer, two mischievous children who made Dennis the Menace look like a wimp, starred in the "Katzenjammer Kids," a popular comic strip first drawn by Rudolph Dirks in 1897.

a cat-lick and a promise: A superficial, slipshod job done with the promise of a more thorough performance at some later date. Although cats are known as fastidious animals, their method of cleaning themselves by licking their paws gave rise to *cat-lick* around 1450, meaning "to superficially clean something instead of thoroughly washing it."

cat's meow: Something splendid or perfect. A slang term popular in the Roaring Twenties, *the cat's meow* doesn't really mean anything but makes a bit more sense than an equivalent slang phrase of the same period, *the cat's pajamas*.

cat's-paw: A person used as a dupe or tool by another to accomplish a purpose. An ancient fable tells the story of a monkey who came upon some chestnuts roasting in a fire. Lacking the means to retrieve the tasty chestnuts from the fire, the clever monkey managed to convince a somewhat dim cat to reach into the flames with his paw and fetch them. The monkey got his chestnuts, the cat was rewarded with a nasty hotfoot, and a metaphor for "chump" was born.

like herding cats: Said of an impossibly complicated or frustrating task. Cats, unlike sheep, cows, and voters, cannot be herded.

looking like something the cat dragged in: Having a full-body bad hair day; appearing bedraggled and disheveled. Domesticated cats' prowess as hunters is matched only by their curious habit of presenting their human companions with the badly battered fruits of their labor, often deposited on the living room floor.

playing cat and mouse: To harass and torment a weaker opponent in a prolonged and playful fashion, from the behavior of a cat that releases a mouse it has caught and injured in order to amuse itself by catching the mouse again. The phrase itself is probably as old as domesticated cats.

pussyfoot: To proceed softly or warily like a cat, since about 1903. Unlike the neutral *cat-foot* (see *cat burglar*), *pussyfoot* carries connotations of timidity and evasiveness, characteristics more often found in politicians than in cats.

salver

Q: I recently received a mail-order catalog offering, among other things I don't need, "vintage salvers" gleaned from the "famous clubs of West End London." The salvers are small silver plates, each bearing the club's insignia. At $150 per plate, I don't plan on buying too many of these, but I'm curious: where does the term *salver* come from?

—*K. W., Columbus, Ohio.*

Well, let's hold on a moment. When you really stop to think about just what's involved in the catalog's obtaining those salvers, the price doesn't seem so unreasonable. After all, there's the special dinner jacket with extra-deep pockets to be commissioned, and the bribe to the club steward, and don't forget the rental for the getaway car. At least that's how I got mine. They're perfect for feeding the cats, incidentally. They make the little fellows feel really special.

Of course, the whole point of salvers is to make someone feel special, whether a household pet or a doddering London club member being served his brandy on one. Most of us only encounter the broad, flat plates called *salvers* at parties, where they are often used to serve canapés or appetizers.

The word *salver* itself comes from the French *salve,* in turn based on the Latin *salvare,* meaning "to save." You sometimes hear that salvers are so named because they "save" one's clothes or carpet from spills, but the actual derivation is slightly more dramatic than that. Salvers were originally the platters used to serve food or drink to a monarch after it had been sampled by the official court taster and certified as free of poison.

Official tasters have become passé in the last century or so, but perhaps they'll make a comeback now that scientists have decided that almost everything we eat is bad for us, even if it isn't deliberately poisoned. I just hope my cats don't get the idea that I'm going to start testing their food for them. It's their job to test mine.

sandboy, happy as a

Q: I have known the expression *happy as a sandboy* for many years but have only recently had cause to wonder about its origin. The *Shorter Oxford English Dictionary* was not of much help, suggesting that a sandboy was possibly one who made a living by selling sand and included the phrase *as jolly as a sandboy* as an example. Do you have any more definitive information on the origin of *sandboy* and, more important, why they are an archetype of jollity or happiness?

—*Alan D., Salisbury, South Australia.*

I'll tell you a little secret, Alan. As I read your letter, I was beginning to suspect that you were, as we word columnists say, a bit whacked. *Happy as a sandboy?* Uh, yeah, O.K. But then I noticed your address, and all was right again. You're not crazy. You're Australian.

Just kidding, mate. It's not surprising that you've heard the phrase for years and I haven't, because *happy as a sandboy* is a distinctly British (and, by extension, Australian) proverbial phrase dating back to about 1821. The *sandboy* in question was a boy (or more likely a man, *boy* being a diminutive often used at the time to denote a lower-class adult male) who made his living selling bags of sand door-to-door. Although this sounds like the setup to a bad joke, sand selling was quite a lucrative occupation in the early nineteenth century, as sand was used for sanding and scouring floors and sopping up spills and as a floor covering in taverns and shops.

One might reasonably imagine that earning one's living by selling something that could be had for free would be enough to make the sandboys happy, but the phrase *happy as a sandboy* is apparently rooted in the sandboys' legendary fondness for alcohol. In his 1841 novel *The Old Curiosity Shop,* Charles Dickens writes of a pub called the *Jolly Sandboys,* marked by a sign featuring three sandboys knocking back tankards of ale and looking very happy indeed.

Sand selling was quite a lucrative occupation in the early nineteenth century.

Unfortunately, soon after the middle of the nineteenth century, sawdust replaced sand as the floor covering of choice in taverns and shops, and the sandboys, alas, ran out of happiness shortly thereafter.

scab

Q : I'd like to know the origin of *scab* as used to describe a strikebreaker or picket-line crosser.

—*Joseph D., via the Internet.*

Yo, Joseph, get with the program. They're not called *scabs* these days. The preferred euphemism is *replacement workers.*

Chances are that when most of us hear the word *scab,* we think of its most common sense, that of "the crust that forms on top of a wound." That was the original meaning of *scab,* which we borrowed directly from the Old Norse word *skabbr* back in the thirteenth century.

Although any doctor will tell you that a scab is a good thing, since it protects a wound while it is healing, by about 1590 we were using *scab* to mean "a low or despicable person." The logic of this derogatory sense is not entirely clear. It most likely stems from the implication that such a scoundrel might well be afflicted with syphilis, which in its advanced stages causes a scabby skin condition. Incidentally, *sceabb,* an Old English word related to *scab,* eventually became *shab,* which originally meant "covered with scabs" but today is used only in the form *shabby* to mean "run-down."

Since *scab* was already being used to mean "lowlife creep," it's not surprising that by the late eighteenth century it was being applied to any worker who refused to join (or actively subverted) an organized trade union movement. As one contemporary source explained in 1792, "What is a scab? He is to

SCAB

The great unionizing drives of the 1930s transformed
SCAB from industrial slang into a household word.

his trade what a traitor is to his country. . . . He first sells the
journeymen, and is himself afterwards sold in his turn by the
masters, till at last he is despised by both and deserted by all."

By the nineteenth century, *scab* was being used, primarily
in the United States, to mean "a worker willing to cross picket
lines to replace a striking worker." The great unionizing drives of
the 1930s then transformed this sense of *scab* from industrial
slang into a household word.

sea change

Q: I hope you can help me on this one. In the last couple
of weeks, I've heard the term *sea change* (or *c change*) on
various news reports. Any idea on a definition and origin?

—*Bill F., via the Internet.*

The proper form is indeed *sea change,* and I've been hearing it a lot lately, too. It seems to have become a favorite buzz
phrase on those Sunday morning TV punditfests, where a bunch
of "commentators" sit around prattling about a "sea change" in
the American electorate or in some politician's campaign strategy.

Sea change, which means "a profound change or transformation in the nature of something," was coined, as were many of our best English words and phrases, by William Shakespeare. The relevant passage in his play *The Tempest* is worth quoting in full, both as an illustration of the original sense of the term and for its remarkable and eerie beauty:

> Full fathom five thy father lies,
>   Of his bones are coral made:
> Those are pearls that were his eyes:
>   Nothing of him that doth fade,
> But doth suffer a sea-change
> Into something rich and strange.

By *sea-change* (which seems to have lately lost its hyphen in common usage) Shakespeare meant "a radical, fundamental transformation," metaphorically similar to the change wrought by prolonged submersion underwater. The English language itself, for instance, is often said to have undergone a sea change when it was imported to the New World, gaining new words and idioms and becoming, to British ears at least, "something rich and strange."

It pains me, however, to hear constant yammering about "sea changes" coming from Washington, where so few things ever actually change. The only genuine sea change I can imagine in connection with politicians would also involve the phrase "full fathom five."

It pains me to hear constant yammering about "SEA CHANGES" coming from Washington, where so few things ever actually change.

shiftless

Q : In a recent conversation, a friend asked the meaning of the word *shiftless*. Upon telling him that it was a derogatory term meaning "lacking responsibility," my boyfriend chimed in that he thought the word came from the concept of "not having a shift," that is, being without a job. This does make sense and fits squarely with the definition, but is it actually accurate? —*Katie H., via the Internet.*

Oh, accurate, schmaccurate, I always say. As long as it makes sense, it works for me. And speaking of working for me, which one of you crazy kids needs a job? I'm looking for a research assistant who also enjoys mowing lawns. It's not really a lawn, actually, more of a six-acre fen full of snakes. But hey, it's not just a job. It's an adventure.

I sense from your question that you suspect that your boyfriend's explanation might be a little too simple (boyfriends are like that), and if so, you're correct. But he's not too far from the truth. The *shifts* in *night shift* and *shiftless* are indeed related, but the relationship is a bit convoluted.

Shift is one of those pesky English words that are so old that they have had time to develop plenty of meanings. In the beginning was the Old English *sciftan,* which came from prehistoric German and meant "to arrange." Once it arrived in English in the fourteenth century, *shift* came to mean "a movement" or "a change." This meaning of "a change" gave us our modern use of *shift* to denote "a specific period of work marked by a change of workers."

Shift kept evolving, however. One of its later meanings, arising in the sixteenth century, was "an ingenious device," and a bit later still, it took on the general sense of "resourcefulness." Someone who is shiftless, therefore, is someone who lacks resourcefulness and initiative and is probably lazy to boot.

It could, of course, be worse. Another derivative of *shift* describes a person who has too much of this kind of shift, is entirely too resourceful and clever and thus not to be trusted—*shifty.*

SHIFT is one of those pesky English words that are so old that they have had time to develop plenty of meanings.

shrink

Q: My wife is puzzled by the moniker given her chosen profession. She swears that in no way does she "shrink" patients. In fact, she believes her job to be "expanding" people— their options and their abilities. Perhaps this came about from psychologists' and psychiatrists' attempts to reduce a patient's perceived problems to a manageable size? Have you a clue?

—*Carl F., Springfield, Illinois.*

Hmmm. Yes. Of course. I think that examining your letter might be very helpful in understanding your problem. Why do you suppose you decided to write to me? Is there some reason that your wife didn't ask this question herself? How did writing this letter make you feel? Anxious? Resentful? Itchy? Hungry? Do you ever dream about appearing in a newspaper column read by millions of people? What do you think you might do if I keep this up for a while? Oh, all right. There's no need to shout.

I'm actually rather surprised that your wife didn't know why people in her profession (psychiatry, psychotherapy, or psychology, I presume) are often referred to as *shrinks*. Many professions actually seem to take a perverse sort of pride in the barbs society lobs their way—the lawyers I know, for example, tend to be my best source of lawyer jokes.

The slang term *shrink* applied to psychiatrists (and any kind of psychotherapist, on occasion) is a shortened form of *headshrinker,* a derogatory comparison of the profession to primitive tribes who ritually dry and shrink the heads of their slain enemies. The term *shrink* dates back at least to the early 1960s and first showed up in print in Thomas Pynchon's novel *The Crying of Lot 49* in 1966.

The term dates back at least to the early 1960s and first showed up in print in Thomas Pynchon's novel *The Crying of Lot 49* in 1966.

If *headshrinker* seems a bit exotic for a derogatory metaphor, it may help to note that magazine cartoons of the early 1960s were awash in cannibalistic natives, witch doctors, and the like, so the imagery of *shrink* is not all that surprising. And if your wife's feelings are a bit hurt by this revelation of the origins of *shrink,* please share with her the wisdom of my personal psychological counselor, Pogo: "Don't take life so serious —it ain't nohow permanent."

EVAN MORRIS

sideburns

Q: Is it true that sideburns were named eponymously after Ambrose Burnside? What were they called before he popularized them? —*Benjamin D., via the Internet.*

I sense a little skepticism in your question, perhaps a gnawing doubt that the story you've heard about *sideburns* is true. Your wariness is entirely justified because very few word origins are as simple and neat as the stories offered to explain them. In the case of *sideburns,* however, the story is true. *Sideburns,* meaning "a style of whiskers grown to cover all or part of the sides of a man's face," is indeed an eponym, a word formed from someone's proper name, in this case that of U.S. Army general Ambrose Burnside (1824–1881).

General Burnside's lasting contribution turned out to be his novel facial hair.

As a commander of Union troops during the American Civil War, General Burnside amassed a record that was erratic at best and often disastrous. His wartime flubs did not, however, prevent him from later serving three terms as governor of Rhode Island and two terms as a U.S. senator. But General Burnside's lasting contribution turned out to be his novel facial hair, which consisted of a full mustache and cheek whiskers over a cleanly shaven chin. This style was a marked departure from the "hot" fashion of the day, which was to shave everything except the chin whiskers, lending the wearer the look of a male goat (a style known, logically, as a *goatee*).

Since the mustache part of General Burnside's invention was nothing new, the cheek whiskers became known as *Burnsides* and enjoyed a certain vogue among men of the day. (Such lush cheek foliage had been known up until then as *muttonchops*, after their resemblance to a popular cut of meat.)

As the memory of General Burnside faded over the years, the style became known as simply *burnsides,* and soon an interesting linguistic flip-flop occurred. Because *burnsides* had become essentially meaningless, popular usage interpreted the *sides* element to mean the sides of the face, in which case *sideburns* seemed to make more sense, and by about 1887 *sideburns* was becoming the accepted name for whiskers on the sides of a man's face.

silhouette

Q: I've heard somewhere that the word *silhouette* came from a French minister of finance who got in some kind of trouble. They couldn't print his picture in the newspaper of the time and instead printed a filled-in outline of his head, and that's where we came up with the word. Is that true?

—*Kenton C., via the Internet.*

Well, not exactly, but it's pretty close. A silhouette is indeed a portrait consisting only of the outline of a person's profile, usually from the neck up, filled in with black. No one knows who invented the basic technique of such shadow painting, which isn't surprising, considering that shadow paintings

Shadow paintings have been found
on the walls of prehistoric caves.

have been found on the walls of prehistoric caves. But we do know the story of how such paintings came to be known as *silhouettes*.

Shortly after Étienne de Silhouette was appointed finance minister of France in 1759, he had what he thought was a really bright idea. With a little fiddling and a slew of new taxes, Étienne thought, he'd be able to rationalize France's national budget and drag the country out of the bankruptcy it had sunk into after the Seven Years' War. Unfortunately, Silhouette made the mistake of slapping some of his heaviest taxes on the nobility, and a scant nine months later he found himself, not surprisingly, unemployed.

During his brief tenure, however, the public perception of Silhouette as a no-fun penny-pincher had made his name a household word, and not a nice one, either. Anything made at low cost by cutting corners was known as *à la Silhouette* (in the manner of Silhouette), which had become a popular synonym for "on the cheap." So it wasn't long before simple shadow portraits, which could be had for a fraction of the cost of having a real portrait painted, came to be known as portraits *à la silhouette* and eventually simply as *silhouettes*.

sincere

Q: Do you know the etymology of the word *sincere* or *sincerity?* I thought that I read somewhere that *sincere* was Latin for "with wax." I've also heard that columns were often made hollow, but ones filled with wax were said to be *sincere,* hence more solid and stable.

—*Barbara C., via the Internet.*

Well, you've come to the right place with your question. Among my friends I just happen to be known as Mr. Sincerity, a title I've painstakingly cultivated over the years by the simple expedient of disagreeing with anything anybody says. It's amazing how many people assume that you're being brutally honest when you're really only being persistently obnoxious.

I don't know about that "columns filled with wax" theory, however. I've tried filling my own columns with all sorts of odd materials—eccentric relatives, vaguely disturbing personal anecdotes—and it hasn't made them one whit more solid or stable.

I think that the theory you've heard about *sincere* and Roman columns is actually a mutation of a very popular (but probably untrue) story based on tracing *sincere* back to the Latin words *sine* (without) and *cera* (wax). Unscrupulous Roman stoneworkers, the story goes, would sometimes cut corners by applying a thick coating of shiny wax to marble rather than taking the time to polish it properly. So widespread was this

EVAN MORRIS

shabby practice, it is said, that honest stoneworkers had to advertise their wares as being *sine cera,* "without wax," to reassure their customers. *Sincere,* the story goes, eventually came to be used more generally to mean "honest" and "straightforward."

While this lovely story is not absolutely impossible, it turns out to be something worse—unnecessary. Most authorities trace *sincere* back to a different Latin word: *sincerus,* meaning "whole" or "pure." Probably based on the roots *sin* (one) and *crescere* (to grow), *sincerus* originally referred to a plant that was of pure stock—not a mixture or hybrid—and later came to mean "anything genuine and not adulterated."

It's amazing how many people assume that you're being brutally honest when you're really only being persistently obnoxious.

soup to nuts

Q: I presume the phrase *soup to nuts* originated with the traditional seven-course meal, beginning with the soup and ending with fruit and nuts. However, where did the seven-course meal originate? Louis XIV's court, perhaps? I would appreciate your insight on the origin of the phrase, since many of the computer software developers are using the term to describe their services. —*Frank W., via the Internet.*

Yeah, I'll just bet they are. What they don't tell you is that the "learning curve" for using their software actually loops

I'm not sure when the classic seven-course dinner was invented, although I know for a fact that I wasn't invited.

gracefully from the point early on when you first realize that you're deep in the soup to the point when, hours later, you finally go completely nuts. It's gotten to the point where consumers are (I kid you not) banding together and threatening to sue computer and software companies for falsely advertising their products as easy to use. Personally, I'm preparing to take advantage of this backlash by investing in typewriter repair courses and slide rule stocks.

As a metaphor for "from beginning to end" or "the whole range of things," *soup to nuts* refers, as you say, to the full course of an elaborate meal, beginning with soup, proceeding through the various courses, and ending, at least in this case, with nuts. I'm not sure when the classic seven-course dinner was invented, although I know for a fact that I wasn't invited. Although *soup to nuts* dates back only to the middle of the twentieth century, similar sayings have been in use since the sixteenth century. The only difference in the various incarnations of this metaphor seems to be in what was considered to constitute a full meal in each historical period. In the seventeenth century, for instance, the whole shebang would be summed up with the phrase *eggs to apples*. And, of course, unless Americans wean themselves from fast food pretty quickly, future generations will probably be hearing a new version of the phrase: *Whoppers to Häagen-Dazs.*

spend a penny

Q: An Englishman visited us, and he said, "I am going to spend a penny." We forgot to ask him what he meant by that. Any ideas? —*Paul and Ruth H., via the Internet.*

Well, I think we can solve this puzzle by staging a little dramatic reenactment—you know, just the way they do on the TV show *Unsolved Mysteries*. Of course, their mysteries all remain unsolved, but that just proves they're not doing it right. Anyway, I'll play your visiting Englishman, sitting on your couch. "I say," I say, "I'm going to spend a penny." And then I leave the room. Now look sharp: where did I go? That's right, I trotted down the hall to your bathroom.

From this simple exercise, we can logically conclude that *going to spend a penny* is a euphemistic British colloquialism for visiting the bathroom, or, as they call it in England, the *W.C.* (for *water closet*) or *loo*. The phrase dates back to the 1940s, when the price of admission to many public lavatories in Britain was, in fact, a penny. Although pay toilets were every bit as common in America during the same period, *spend a penny* has never been heard much over here.

Far more common is the announcement by someone in a social setting that he (or, less frequently, she) has to *go see a man about a dog* (or *a horse*). There's usually no dog or horse involved, of course, and there

The phrase dates back to the 1940s, when the price of admission to many public lavatories in Britain was, in fact, a PENNY.

probably never was. *See a man about a dog* first showed up in the middle of the nineteenth century as an all-purpose excuse to leave the room, and during Prohibition here in the United States, it often meant "I'm going to go have a drink."

Incidentally, in case you folks out there were just warming up your ballpoints to write and ask where the term *loo* came from, I have some bad news: no one knows for sure. The most likely theory traces it to the French noun *lieu* (place), possibly from a shortening of the phrase *lieux d'aisance,* meaning "places of comfort" (or "comfort stations").

straw boss

Q: What does the term *straw boss* mean, and where did it originate? —*Larry M., via the Internet.*

Call me a clueless city slicker (preferably behind my back, lest I spend the next two weeks sulking in the chicken coop), but there are some pretty basic elements of rural living that have long mystified me. I distinctly remember sitting on the New York City subway several years ago, for instance, and wondering what the difference between straw and hay was. Any New Yorker will understand why pondering such a seemingly irrelevant matter was safer than trying to imagine why the guy riding next to me had lined his hat with tinfoil.

Anyway, only last summer, when I was seated on an actual bale of straw at a rural picnic, did it occur to me to ask my hosts to explain the difference. Hay, I was told, is usually just dried grass, sometimes with a little alfalfa thrown in, used as feed for horses and cattle. Straw, on the other hand, is the stalks of wheat or other grains left over after harvesting the good parts and is used primarily for livestock bedding. Needless to say, immediately upon learning this I skedaddled to the nearest telephone and canceled the bunk beds my own cows had convinced me to order for them. I am also reconsidering the need for cable TV in the barn.

Since straw is fundamentally a by-product of the real business of a farm, it's not surprising to learn that *straw boss* does not mean the "big boss" of any job, but rather "an assistant or subordinate boss, usually on the level of the foreman of a work crew." The term is said to have arisen from the usual arrangement of workers threshing wheat in the fields. The primary boss would be in charge of the wheat entering the threshing apparatus, while the assistant, or "straw," boss would supervise the crew gathering and baling the straw that the thresher discarded. *Straw boss* first appeared in print in the late nineteenth century, and quickly became a metaphor for any low-level supervisor. And since straw bosses rarely wield any real power aside from the ability to make those under them miserable, *straw boss* today is often a synonym for "a petty and vindictive superior."

STRAW BOSSES rarely wield any real power aside from the ability to make those under them miserable.

Go Figure . . .

Of all the languages that have lent their words to modern English, perhaps none is so expressive as Yiddish. Born in the Jewish ghettos of Europe and incorporating elements of Hebrew, German, Russian, Polish, and several other languages, Yiddish often puts into one or two words what "formal English" would take several sentences to explain and usually does it with both keen insight into human nature and a healthy dose of self-deprecating humor. As the late Leo Rosten pointed out in his classic *The Joys of Yiddish*, Yiddish is far more than just a vocabulary: it's a whole way of speaking. The proper pronunciation and emphasis of Yiddishisms is often key to their effectiveness, as is the unusual structure ("This I need?") of many Yiddish phrases.

The integration of many Yiddishisms into mainstream English has been so complete that many of our Yiddish-derived figures of speech are rarely recognized as such. But if you've ever said "Get lost," "All right, already," or "O.K. by me," you've been using Yiddishisms. Following are a few more that have made it into the mainstream.

maven: From the Hebrew *mevin*, meaning "understanding." A maven (rhymes with "raven") is not just someone who knows everything there is to know about a subject, be it wine or cigars or stereo systems; a maven is a connoisseur, a devotee, a disciple of his or her passion. Experts have opinions. A maven knows the truth.

megillah: Yiddish slang for a long, complicated, and often boring story. *Megillah* comes from the Hebrew word for "scroll," referring to the five books of the Old Testament. One of them, the Book of Esther, is the original whole megillah in the slang sense.

mensch: In German, *mensch* simply means "person," but in Yiddish slang, a mensch (rhymes with "bench") is someone whose strength of character, generosity, or courage make him or her a truly outstanding human being. The bus driver who returns a lost briefcase is a mensch, as is the rich man who gives his money to charity, as is the child who stands up to the schoolyard bully. Unfortunately, mensches, being both modest and honest by nature, almost never run for public office.

meshuga: "Crazy" in Hebrew. Also *meshuggener* (crazy man) and *meshuggeneh* (crazy woman). Can be used either seriously (the meshuga person is truly mentally ill) or lightly (the meshuga person loans his wife's brother large sums of money). A similar word, *mishegoss* (meaning "insanity"), is always used lightly.

schlock: Anything cheap, cheesy, or fake. *Schlock* (rhymes with "lock") comes from the German *schlag,* meaning "a blow," probably because schlocky merchandise has often been knocked around or damaged. A store that specializes in schlock is known as a *schlock house,* and the proprietor is known as a *schlockmeister* (from the German *meister,* or "master").

schmaltz: Literally, chicken fat, a staple of Old World Jewish cuisine. In a slang sense, *schmaltz* also means the kind of gooey sentimentality often found in movies starring talking farm animals or in "very special episodes" of TV sitcoms.

schmooze: A heart-to-heart talk, from the Hebrew *shmuos* (things heard). In popular usage, *schmoozing* means "casually trading gossip and shooting the breeze with friends."

tchotchke: Yiddish (pronounced "CHOCH-kah") for a trinket or toy, the kind of thing tourists bring back from vacation, from a Slavic word meaning "to play pranks." *Tchotchke* (also spelled *tsatske*) can sometimes mean "a small gift or reward," "an inconsequential person," or even "a pretty girl." The plural of *tchotchke* is *tchotchkies,* which is good to know because nobody has just one tchotchke.

sundae

Q: How did the sundae—a confection made up of ice cream, a sticky, sweet sauce, and whipped cream, topped with crushed nuts and a cherry—get its name? Does its spelling have anything to do with blue laws, which restrict commerce on Sundays?   —*Kate P., via the Internet.*

Funny you should ask. I was driving through Baltimore, Ohio (population 3,000), a while back, when an illuminated sign in front of a small church caught my eye. WE'RE NOT BASKIN-ROBBINS, it declared to an audience of bored cows, BUT OUR SUNDAYS ARE DIVINE. I suspect that whatever local wit came up with that knee-slapper was operating on the presumption that *Sunday* and *sundae* are unrelated and only coincidentally homophones (words that sound the same). But *sundae* is, according to lexicographic authorities, definitely related to *Sunday*. The only problem is that no one seems to know exactly what the connection is.

We do know that *sundae* is an American invention, and although accounts of the invention of the dish itself vary, folks were eating sundaes as early as 1897. One popular story about the origin of the name *sundae* traces it to an ice cream purveyor in Manitowoc, Wisconsin, named George Giffy. It is said that Giffy sold his most special concoctions only on Sunday at first, and that even after public demand forced him to sell them every day, he continued to call them *Sundays* or *sundaes*.

The odd spelling of *sundae* has also been fodder for a variety of theories. The dish has gone by other names at various times, most notably *sundi* and the very weird *sondhi*. Some accounts have explained all these variants as attempts to avoid offending the sensibilities of the devoutly religious, who might take a dim view of a pile of ice cream and syrup being named after their Sabbath. If this theory is true, whoever came up with the modified spelling *sundae* probably never dreamt that they were also supplying the setup for more than a century of lame puns.

The dish has gone by other names at various times, most notably *sundi* and the very weird *sondhi*.

swanny/swan

Q: I'm from the South. I use and hear the expression "Well, I Swanee." How did this come into being? It has to do with the Swanee River, I'm sure.

— *Susie, via the Internet.*

Well, maybe a little. It all depends on how strictly you mean "has to do with."

Before we begin, I must admit that I'm not precisely sure where the Swanee River is. This admission should not be taken as a disparagement of the South in any way. I am similarly uncertain of the exact location of Minnesota. Anyway, I'm sure the Swanee is down there somewhere. And I have no doubt that it's a lovely river, otherwise Stephen Foster would not have featured it in his immortal song "Old Folks at Home" ("Way down upon the Swanee River, / Far, far away, / There's where my heart is" something something something . . .). But, logical as your theory may seem, the Swanee River is not the source of *I swanny.*

For that we must travel to the north of England, where when folks really wanted other folks to believe something they were saying, they would preface it with *I shall warrant ye,* meaning "I swear to you that this is true." Of course, accents in the north of England being thicker than wool soaked in molasses, what they actually said was closer to *I's wan ye,* which sounds a great deal like *I swanny.* It was in this *I swanny* form that the phrase was imported into the United States in the mid–nineteenth century, although an even briefer form, *I swan,* is perhaps more popular in this country. Today *I swanny* and *I swan* are most often used as interjections or expressions of surprise, as in "Ruth really ran off with that cute UPS guy? Well, I swan!"

Meanwhile, back at the Swanee River, wherever it may be, what you regard as a natural connection with *I swanny* is really just a fortunate coincidence. But the presumable proximity of the Swanee River has almost certainly preserved a charming but archaic expression that otherwise might well have become as extinct in the South as it is in the rest of the United States.

The Swanee River is not the source of I SWANNY.

EVAN MORRIS

tawdry

Q: I was shopping with a friend, and she described one dress I liked as "tawdry." Where did this word come from? —*E. F., via the Internet.*

Your friend said this? Don't look now, but you seem to be harboring a fugitive from the Tact Police. I'll bet she didn't buy anything herself because she's saving up for charm school.

In any case, your friend is no Queen Etheldreda, who was monarch of Northumbria, in what is now northern England, in the seventh century. Etheldreda, also known as Audrey (who can blame her?), was a kind and generous queen, famous for her good deeds and charity. After she ran away from her husband, who was not kind and generous, she founded an abbey and devoted the rest of her life to helping the common people. Her only vanity was a passion

St. Audrey's Lace was slurred into TAWDRY LACE, *via a common linguistic process called elision.*

for fine scarves and necklaces, and when she was stricken with throat cancer, she regarded the disease as divine punishment for her devotion to showy neckwear. After her death she was canonized, and the villagers nearby established an annual festival in her honor. Among other wares merchants sold at the fair were beautiful scarves in tribute to Saint Audrey. Originally the scarves were of the finest lace, and St. Audrey's lace became the most desirable in Britain. Eventually, two things happened, both fairly inevitable, given human nature. First, *St. Audrey's lace* was slurred into *tawdry lace,* via a common linguistic process called *elision*. Still, *tawdry* continued to mean "refined" for several hundred years. But eventually, the quality of the product was degraded by unscrupulous vendors until the word *tawdry,* once a tribute to a kind and selfless saint, became a synonym for "something cheap and worthless pretending to be of value."

teddy

Q: Since it's getting close to Valentine's Day as I write this, I've had women's lingerie on my mind (perhaps more than usual). Wandering around the store, I encountered the ubiquitous teddy. How did this garment get its name?

— *Scott S., via the Internet.*

Hoo boy. Where to begin? First of all, I must caution you that the occasion to which you refer is no longer properly known as *Valentine's Day* (much less *Saint Valentine's Day*). It now goes by the far less inflammatory (I guess) moniker *Special Person Day,* at least in a few fiercely sensitive public school districts. Don't get me started. And second, if things have reached the point where you can blithely refer to "the ubiquitous teddy," I suspect that "casual day" wherever you work has gone way too far.

The *Oxford English Dictionary* (an excellent source for lingerie information, I'll have you know) defines *teddy* as "a woman's undergarment combining chemise and panties," evidently popular among women as what the *OED* terms *sleepwear*.

The TEDDY is named, of course, for
President Theodore Roosevelt, who routinely
wore one to cabinet meetings.

The whole effect, I am told, is something like a short, loose, lacy smock.

The teddy is named, of course, for President Theodore Roosevelt, who routinely wore one to cabinet meetings. No, wait, that was J. Edgar Hoover. But Teddy Roosevelt does loom large in *teddy* lore. President Roosevelt was notably fond of bear hunting, a fact that was the subject of an enormously popular humorous poem published in the *New York Times* in 1906 featuring two bears named *Teddy B.* and *Teddy G.* Savvy toy dealers soon began marketing stuffed toy bears advertised as *Teddy Bears,* and the ensuing teddy bear fad continues to this day.

All of which brings us back (as all historical discussions must) to lingerie. The teddy is thought to have been so christened back in the 1920s because its somewhat shapeless puffiness reminded someone (who must have *really* needed new glasses) of the general outlines of a teddy bear.

three sheets to the wind

Q: I have always been intrigued by the phrase *three sheets to the wind,* to describe someone being drunk. Most people I have asked feel it has its origins with sailors. Is there any truth to that? If it were *three sails to the wind,* I could see it.

—*David K., via the Internet.*

Here we go again. I suppose we all have our little self-destructive habits. Moths stand in line to get to the flame, perfectly rational people join mail-order book clubs, and I answer questions having to do with boats. The problem is that, although I am usually 99 percent right when I answer a query involving seafaring terms, I always seem to flub some tiny detail, bringing the crusty wrath of several hundred deeply offended sea dogs down on my head. If anyone has ever wondered what retired sailors do to pass the time, I have your answer: they lie in wait for me to screw up.

So, having battened down my hatches, I'll just lash myself to the main-mizzen (or whatever) and shout a hearty "You betcha!" The phrase *three sheets to the wind* does indeed come from the world of seafaring, specifically sailing ships. The sheets referred to in the phrase are not sails but ropes. Of course, the first thing one learns about ropes once aboard ship is that they are never called *ropes.* They are named according to their particular function: *halyards* (which move or hold things vertically, usually sails), *sheets* (which move or hold things horizontally), and *lines* (which hold things in a static position). The sheets in this case are those ropes that hold the sails in place. If one sheet is loose, the sail will flap in the wind, and the ship's progress will be unsteady. Two sheets loose ("to the wind"), and you have a

The phrase does indeed come from the world of seafaring, specifically sailing ships.

major problem, and with three sheets to the wind, the ship reels like a drunken sailor.

The specific number of sheets in the phrase wasn't random, by the way—there was, at one time, a sort of rating system of inebriation among sailors, according to which *one sheet* meant "tipsy," and so on, up to *four sheets to the wind,* which meant "completely unconscious."

Tin Pan Alley

Q : I teach a course in jazz history at McGill University, and I was talking about how musicians like Charlie Parker and Dizzy Gillespie used to take tunes written by Tin Pan Alley composers (Gershwin, Porter, Eubie Blake, Irving Berlin, etc.) and write new melodies on the old harmonies. One of the students asked, "Where does the phrase *Tin Pan Alley* come from?" I'm stumped. Not one music teacher I've spoken to has any idea. Can you help?

—*Andre W., via the Internet.*

Well, I'll give it a shot—can you hum a few bars? Actually, I'll make you a deal. I'll explain where *Tin Pan Alley* comes from if you'll explain where all the tunes went. I hate to sound like a cranky old geezer, but nothing written since about 1980 strikes me as even remotely hummable.

Linguistically, the term is a synecdoche—a specific thing or place that comes to stand for a broader category.

SYNECDOCHE

Tin Pan Alley is, and has been for many years, a popular term for the music industry, especially the songwriting and publishing part of it, as opposed to the recording industry. Linguistically, the term *Tin Pan Alley* is a *synecdoche*—a specific thing or place that comes to stand for a broader category, as the term *Wall Street* stands for the world of high finance and the stock market in general, and *Madison Avenue* is often used as shorthand for the advertising industry. Like Wall Street and Madison Avenue, Tin Pan Alley is a real place in New York City: the side streets in the area of the Times Square theatrical district, where music publishers have their offices and many of the great songwriters, as you note, have plied their trade. The New York songwriting district has been known as Tin Pan Alley since the late 1880s, although it actually started out a bit further downtown and only drifted up to its present location in the 1920s.

Tin Pan Alley owes its name, logically enough, to a bit of late-nineteenth-century musicians' slang. A *tin pan* or *tin-panny* was a cheap piano, so-called because its shallow, tinny tone was likened to beating on a tin pan. If you can imagine a summer's day on Tin Pan Alley at the turn of the century, filled with the cacophony of tin-pannies wafting from the open office windows of a hundred music publishers, you'll see why *Tin Pan Alley* was such a perfect name for the New York music business.

EVAN MORRIS

twilight

Q: My brother and I were traveling one evening just as the sun was setting over the horizon. Roused by an inexplicable curiosity, I turned to my brother and asked if it was twilight or dusk. He didn't know. Then I asked which comes first. Is it twilight before it's evening? Is it dusk after twilight? He didn't know. Can you shed some light on this topic? What's the difference between *dusk, twilight, sunset,* and *evening?* Do they all mean the same thing?

—Merrysarie, via the Internet.

My, we have a lot of questions, don't we? I'm surprised your brother didn't jettison you by the roadside. Poor guy's trying to watch a pretty sunset, and you're badgering him with an impromptu vocabulary test.

The broadest (and vaguest) of the terms you're asking about is *evening,* which generally refers to the period of time between sunset and whenever you get around to going to sleep. *Evening* is derived from the archaic noun *even,* from the Old English word *aefen,* meaning "lateness."

Sunset itself simply means "the time that the sun sets, or sinks below the horizon." (*Set* in this sense is closely related to the verb *sit.*)

Twilight comes right after sunset, when the sun is below the horizon but the sky is still illuminated by its light refracted

in the earth's atmosphere. The Old English word *twi* meant "half," "two," or "between," so *twilight* means "the period between daylight and darkness." Strictly speaking, however, *twilight* can also refer to the half-light period just before morning sunrise.

Dusk means "the later stage of evening twilight," when it is getting really dark, and probably comes from the Old English word *dox,* which meant, logically enough, "dark." Again, *dusk* can also mean "the early stages of morning twilight before sunrise," but using the word that way will only confuse everyone, so please don't.

The bottom line is that evening begins with sunset. Twilight comes after the sun actually sets and progresses to dusk just before things go completely dark.

tycoon

Q: I found myself referring to someone as a "tycoon" the other day, and suddenly the word seemed very archaic to me. Do we still have tycoons today? Where did the word come from, anyway?

—*Kathy M., Brooklyn, New York.*

After considering your question for a moment, I think you may be onto something. Where have all the tycoons gone? Why don't we see public service announcements exhorting us to save the tycoons by preserving their natural habitats, Nob Hill and Grosse Point? Are we to be left with nothing but those dreadful "entrepreneurs" (which, I believe, is French for "watch your wallet")? It is indeed a tragedy.

Many of us remember when tycoons roamed the land in great, lumbering herds (not me, of course, but I've heard the stories). *Tycoon* comes to us from Japanese, where a *taikun* was a military leader or shogun. The word was adopted into American English around the middle of the nineteenth century and was popularized, surprisingly enough, as a nickname for Abraham Lincoln, not commonly thought of as an overbearing sort of fellow. *Tycoon* only came to be applied to businessmen after World War I.

Tycoons in their heyday were notable for getting exactly what they wanted, whether it made sense or not. Bill Bryson, in his history of the English language in the United States, *Made in America*, illustrates what being a tycoon meant in the early twentieth century: "The servants at J. P. Morgan's London residence nightly prepared dinner, turned down the bed, and laid out nightclothes for their master even when he was known beyond doubt to be three thousand miles away in New York. . . . James Gordon Bennett, a newspaper baron, liked to announce his arrival in a restaurant by yanking the tablecloths from all the tables he passed. He would then hand the manager a wad of cash with which to compensate his victims for their lost meals and spattered attire." Now *that's* a tycoon. Perhaps that's also why they're extinct.

The word was popularized, surprisingly enough, as a nickname for Abraham Lincoln.

utopia

Q: *Utopia* means "no place," right? How old is this term, and who were the first persons to name entities that they cannot see, those beyond empirical data?

— *Christine M., via the Internet.*

Good evening, ladies and gentlemen, and welcome to another episode of *Entities beyond Empirical Data,* also known as *Things That Go Bump in the Dictionary.* Tonight's episode: "The Road to Utopia, or You Can't Get There from Here."

To answer your second question first: people have been assigning names to things that they cannot see (which may not exist in the first place) since time immemorial, which, in round figures, was gazillions of years ago. After all, the ability to imagine things not immediately in front of one, whether it be dinner or a Supreme Being, is the hallmark of the human animal, along with a passion for naming things, both seen and unseen. This marvelous ability has given us all the fruits of great human cultures—art, religion, music, literature, poetry, *Monday Night Football,* and television infomercials. You name it, and folks can imagine it (and then name it). Personally, judging by those last two, I think it's time to stop.

People have been assigning names to things that they cannot see (which may not exist in the first place) since time immemorial.

In the case of *utopia,* the namer was Sir Thomas More, an English humanist philosopher, in 1516. In his book *Utopia,* More contrasted the state of life in

Europe at that time with conditions in an imaginary ideal society he called *Utopia*, from the Greek *ou* ("no" or "not") and *topos* (place). By naming his ideal world "nowhere," More indicated that such a place was impossible and that the alternative, improving our existing society, was our only choice.

Human beings are not the best listeners in the animal kingdom, however, and many people over the years have attempted to forcibly erect actual "utopian societies," usually with remarkably unpleasant and dramatically un-utopian results. Such experiments are more properly known as *dystopias,* from the Greek *dys,* meaning "bad" or "ill."

vet

Q: For many years I have wondered about the origins of a word bandied about by all those political wonks and columnists out there: *vet*. My understanding is that it means "to fully investigate someone's background"—to find out, for example, whether they hired illegal nannies, inhaled their marijuana, and so forth. Is the word merely a corruption of *investigate?* Or is there a deeper, more sinister story to the origins of this word? Please vet it out for me.

—*SPS, via the Internet.*

Well, golly, SPS (can I call you S for short?), there's always a deeper, more sinister story, isn't there? It just takes years

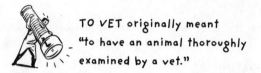

TO VET originally meant "to have an animal thoroughly examined by a vet."

to come out sometimes. How many of us, for instance, would ever have suspected that . . . hold on a moment. They don't know that yet? Yikes. Well, never mind, folks, it's not important. On with the column.

You're absolutely right in your guess that to *vet* means "to examine something or someone in a painstaking fashion," with what an older cliché would call a *fine-tooth comb*. In current usage, to *vet* means "to examine someone's background for offenses that might later prove embarrassing or (in bureaucratese) might compromise security."

Vet has only fairly recently become the word du jour among magazine writers and political pundits in the United States, which explains why you hear it so often these days. But while *vet* evidently seems exotic to reporters and editorialists on this side of the Atlantic, it has been in standard, albeit informal, use in Britain since the turn of the century.

Perhaps the most surprising thing about *vet* is its origin, because it seems almost too simple. *Vet,* the verb, like *vet* the noun, is a shortening of *veterinarian,* and *to vet* originally meant "to have an animal thoroughly examined by a vet." *Veterinarian,* in turn, comes from the Latin *veterinae,* or "cattle," which constituted the bulk of early veterinarians' patients. So if you feel like livestock next time the IRS vets your tax return, just do as I do: open your big brown eyes and moo.

Welsh rabbit

Q : I was grocery shopping with my mother last week, and as we passed the soup section, she asked me to grab her a can of "Welsh rabbit." I thought she was kidding, because the can was clearly labeled *Welsh rarebit* (and that's how I've always heard it said), but she said that *rabbit* was right and *rarebit* was wrong. Is she right? What has cheddar cheese soup got to do with rabbits? —*Doris M., via the Internet.*

Remember when you were little and it seemed like your mother was always right? Well, brace yourself: your mother is right again.

The proper name of the dish is *rabbit,* as in the hopping critter with big ears. Both the dish and its name date back to the eighteenth century, and its name reflects the eternal (so far) national rivalry between England and Wales. Some wag, almost certainly English, christened the popular but humble dish of melted cheese over toast *Welsh rabbit,* much in the same nationalistic spirit as frogs were known as *Dutch nightingales* and desertion was known as *taking French leave.* The implication, of course, was that the Welsh could not obtain or afford real rabbit and had to make do with this cheesy substitute.

The distinguishing feature of *Welsh rabbit* is that it is a joke, which brings us to where that *rarebit* business came from. Someone, somewhere, simply didn't get the joke. Some humorless

War of Words, Words of War

War—what is it good for? Absolutely nothing, as the song says. Except, apparently, for enriching our language. Because warfare and preparations for war have been depressingly constant features of human history, many of our modern English words, phrases, and figures of speech have strikingly bellicose roots. Even the study of language itself has prompted military metaphors: "A language," goes an old linguist's saw, "is just a dialect with an army."

Just how pervasive military terminology and other "war words" have become in English today is illustrated by how often we use them without a glimmer of their often grim original meanings. Here are a few examples of military words and phrases that have achieved civilian status.

deadline: An absolute time limit or due date by which a task must be accomplished, especially the time by which a newspaper article must be turned in by the reporter to be publishable in the next edition. During the American Civil War, the guards at the notoriously brutal Confederate military prison at Andersonville drew a line on the ground around the perimeter of the compound, a uniform seventeen feet inside the prison walls. Any prisoner crossing over that line was presumed to be trying to reach the wall in order to escape and was summarily shot. This boundary was known succinctly as the *dead line*. The first appearance in print of this original military sense of the term comes in the *Congressional Record* in 1864. *Deadline* in the journalistic sense first showed up around 1920 and quickly jumped into general usage, meaning any sort of absolute, ironclad, "or else" time limit.

martinet: A rigid, demanding, humorless superior. The very first (and possibly worst) martinet was Jean Martinet, a seventeenth-century French army officer famous for his high standards, rigid discipline, and short fuse. General Martinet's passion was getting his men to march hour after hour, perfectly in step, in nice straight ranks. General Martinet's methods eventually became the model of training in most Western armies, but in the civilian world his name became synonymous with "petty dictator."

Pyrrhic victory: A victory in name only. *Pyrrhic* refers to King Pyrrhus of Epirus, who led his troops into battle against the Romans at Ausculum in 279 B.C. Pyrrhus was victorious in this first great clash between the Greeks and the Romans, but at the terrible cost of most of his best troops and officers. Pyrrhus's famous words after the battle, "One more such victory, and we are lost!" established *Pyrrhic victory* as a vivid metaphor for a hollow triumph gained at too high a cost. Oddly enough, this metaphor, based on an event that took place more than two thousand years ago, didn't show up in general English usage until the late nineteenth century. But it has taken off with a vengeance since then, and *Pyrrhic victory* is now a staple of every political analyst's rhetorical arsenal.

scuttlebutt: Rumor; "the word going around." On nineteenth-century British navy warships the scuttlebutt was a large wooden cask with a hole cut in the lid that held the crew's drinking water; the word combines *scuttle* (a hole) and *butt* (a cask). Seamen often exchanged the latest rumors over the scuttlebutt, as modern office workers gathering at the watercooler do today.

turncoat: A traitor; anyone who changes principles or allegiances to the detriment of former friends. The story (perhaps apocryphal) is told of the duke of Saxony, whose land was uncomfortably located between the warring French and Saxons. The duke, according to legend, wore a reversible coat, one side blue (the Saxon color), the other side white (the French color), allowing him to quickly change his display of allegiance should the need arise.

ancient grammarian decided that, since there was clearly no rabbit involved, *rabbit* must be a degenerate form of something, and determined that the missing "proper" name must be *rarebit*. Why anyone would think that the stalwart Welsh would tolerate such a prissy name as *rarebit* for anything is another question, but unfortunately the new sanitized name stuck, at least in the minds of menu writers. Such high-handed pedantry is frustrating indeed for anyone who values the wonderful ability of English phrases such as *Welsh rabbit* to immortalize a joke hundreds of years old. As the eminent English grammarian H. W. Fowler put it in 1926, "*Welsh rabbit* is amusing and right, and *Welsh rarebit* stupid and wrong."

As English grammarian H. W. Fowler put it in 1926, "WELSH RABBIT is amusing and right, and *Welsh rarebit* stupid and wrong."

whole nine yards

Q: What is the origin of the expression *the whole nine yards?* —*Pam G. and the Bichons of Camelot, Livingston, New Jersey.*

Bichons of Camelot? Bichons frises? Fuzzy little white dogs wearing medieval suits of armor? I think I need another cup of coffee.

O.K., I'm back, and the answer to your question about the origin of *the whole nine yards* (meaning "the whole thing" or "everything") is that nobody knows for sure. There are dozens

EVAN MORRIS

of theories about this phrase, many of them passionately held by folks who send them to me at the rate of about ten per week. Not one of these theories, unfortunately, has ever been verified.

Some of the more popular theories trace *the whole nine yards* to the amount of cloth needed to make a wedding dress or bridal train, a man's three-piece suit, a burial shroud, or other apparel. Other theories trace the phrase to the capacity of cement mixers or assert that *yards* actually means "yardarms," the spars on a large sailing ship that actually hold the sails. One theory particularly popular at the moment (judging from my mail) is that machine gun ammunition belts in World War II fighters were nine yards long, so that a pilot who expended all his ammo in a dogfight would have shot "the whole nine yards."

There are difficulties with all these theories. *The whole nine yards* first cropped up in print in the mid-1960s, so any explanations tracing the phrase to sailing ships are unlikely to be true. Nine yards is not a standard amount of material in connection with any garment or cement mixer. And even if machine gun belts really were twenty-seven feet long in World War II, why has the phrase *the whole nine yards* not been found in a single published account of that very well documented war?

The problem here is a lack, not of theories that sound good, but of solid evidence. What we need, and I'd be thrilled to see it, is an example of *the whole nine yards* in print (preferably before the mid-1960s) that uses the phrase in reference to a specific trade or custom, not just in its modern "whole shebang" sense.

NINE YARDS is not a standard amount of material in connection with any garment or cement mixer.

Until somebody supplies that kind of solid citation, I'll be hanging out down on the corner, not holding my breath.

wimp

Q: I am doing a project for my English class and would like to know what the word *wimp* really means and where it came from. —*Anonymous, via the Internet.*

Since I am by nature an optimistic, trusting sort of person, I am going to assume that this is a genuine question and not a snide reference to my behavior upon being attacked by a deranged groundhog in my own driveway last summer. In any case, I would like to note that sound travels great distances out here in the country, so the mere fact that my screams were heard in the next county does not, ipso facto, make me a wimp.

WIMP got a big boost in general usage thanks to a hilarious slip in the *Boston Globe* in 1980.

As the *Oxford English Dictionary* defines the term, *wimp* means "a feeble or ineffectual person; one who is spineless or 'wet.'" (*Wet* is a fine English slang term meaning "inept or dorky.") The folks at *Oxford* go on to note (for the benefit of those who have recently arrived from Mars, I suppose) that *wimp* is "used only as a term of abuse or contempt."

That's putting it mildly. Since *wimp* became popular around 1960, it has been considered synonymous with "drip," "weakling," "dork," "nerd," and "wuss." A standard part of college slang for years, *wimp* got a big boost in general usage thanks to a hilarious slip in the *Boston Globe* in 1980. Somehow a newsroom prank wasn't caught in time, and an editorial analyzing President Jimmy Carter's economic pronouncements went to press under the headline MUSH FROM THE WIMP.

One of the theories proposed for the origin of *wimp* is that it comes from the name of J. Wellington Wimpy, also known as Wimpy, a character in the old "Popeye" cartoons. "I'll gladly pay you Tuesday for a hamburger today" was Wimpy's perennial plaintive refrain, and his whiny, timid demeanor would certainly have made him a good mascot for wimps worldwide.

But a more likely source is simply the word *whimper*, a characteristic activity of wimps. Bolstering this theory is the fact that when *wimp* first appeared in the 1920s in England, it was college slang for "a woman or girl," based on the idea that women are more likely to weep than men.

yahoo

Q: A friend of mine told me that *Yahoo!*, the name of the Web directory, is a word that actually means the same thing as *bozo*. Is this true? Why would they name their Web site after a word that means "idiot"?

—*Larry R., via the Internet.*

Hard to say. At first I suspected that the name *Yahoo!* (the exclamation point is part of their trademark) might be a subtle putdown of the site's users (as in "You'd have to be a yahoo to need us") until I realized that no one would be crazy enough to try to beat Microsoft at the customer-humiliation game. The story I heard when Yahoo! started up way back in 1994 was that the name stood for *yet another hierarchical officious oracle.* But the Yahoo! Web page now says that the name was chosen because the site's two founders, David Filo and Jerry Yang, "considered themselves yahoos." If that's true, they may be the world's richest yahoos.

But whatever the rationale for the Web site's name, your friend is correct about the meaning of the word *yahoo,* which since 1726 has meant "a moronic, loudmouthed, and occasionally violent hooligan." Anyone who remembers the film *Easy Rider* will recognize the good ol' boys who blew away Dennis Hopper and Peter Fonda at the end of the movie as prime examples of yahoos.

The word was invented by Jonathan Swift in his fantastic tale *Gulliver's Travels* in 1726.

We know exactly how old *yahoo* is because the word was invented by Jonathan Swift in his fantastic tale *Gulliver's Travels* in 1726. Late in the book, Gulliver travels to Houyhnhnmland, where he encounters the Yahoos. Human in form, the Yahoos are savage in behavior, described by Swift as cunning, malicious, and treacherous, but also fundamentally cowardly. The rulers of Houyhnhnmland, in contrast, are the Houyhnhnm, a refined, sensitive, and deeply ethical people who just happen to be horses.

(The name *Houyhnhnm,* incidentally, was Swift's rendition of the sound of a horse's whinny.)

So evocative was Swift's depiction of the Yahoos' depravity that *yahoo* almost immediately entered English as a synonym for "an ignorant brute." Over the years, *yahoo* has also often been invoked in the cultural realm, where those who lack an appreciation for the finer points of modern art, for instance, have been accused of being yahoos.

Yankee

Q: How about the word *Yank* or *Yankee?* Where and how did that originate? —*Jeff T., via the Internet.*

The Word Detective slowly climbed the long flight of stairs to his small office in a dingy building on Manhattan's Upper West Side. Wearily, he slumped into his worn desk chair, casually tossed his fedora out the window, and retrieved a dusty bottle from the bottom drawer of his battered desk. Brushing aside a pile of worn-out adverbs, he poured himself a double shot of Old Webster's. "It's the simple questions," he remarked to the large orange cat, who was just awakening from his all-day nap atop a pile of dictionaries, "the simple questions that really drive a guy nuts."

"Listen to this one," he continued, after pausing to refill his glass. "This guy writes me with a question, a slow-pitch softball question, the kind of question any two-bit hick etymologist

*"It's the simple questions," he remarked to the large
orange cat, who was just awakening from his all-day nap
atop a pile of dictionaries, "the simple questions that
really drive a guy nuts."*

should be able to answer with a *Golden Book Children's Dictionary* and a box of crayons." He rubbed his eyes.

"Where does *Yankee* come from? the guy asks me. Piece of cake, right? I round up the usual dictionaries. Know what I find? Nothing. Not a clue. 'Origin unknown,' they all claim. Yeah, right. So I ask around, check my confidential sources. No dice again. Nobody knows. They figure it first showed up in America around the time of the Revolutionary War, but beyond that, the trail goes cold. I check the slang dictionaries. Nada. Zippo. I spend all day plowing through every library in town, and all I've got to show for it is a bunch of half-baked theories and a headache the size of the *Oxford English Dictionary*—the twenty-volume edition."

The cat cleared his throat hesitantly, then suggested, "But what about the Indians? Wasn't there supposedly a Yanko tribe or a word in Cherokee that sounded like *Yankee?*" "Hogwash," the Word Detective growled. "Total rubbish. No such tribe, no such word. Likewise the theory about its being from the Persian word for 'warlike man.' That turned out to be a joke some mug was playing on Noah Webster." He reached for the bottle again, but the cat got there first and drained it. He pretended not to notice. After all, the cat worked cheap.

Night was coming. The Word Detective lit a cigarette, then thought better of it and tossed it into a box of reader mail sitting in the corner. The cat sighed, then brightened. "What about 'Yankee Doodle'? Maybe the word came from the song." "Fuggeddaboudit, chum," the Detective smiled bitterly. "You're thinking cats before kittens. Word first, then song. The only thing interesting about that song is that the redcoats used to sing it to annoy the colonists. But after the minutemen whipped King George at Lexington and Concord, the colonists decided to sing the song themselves. By the time we got to Yorktown, 'Yankee Doodle' had turned into a swan song for the Brits."

The cat laid down ponderously, fell asleep briefly, and promptly rolled off the edge of the desk, landing on the floor with the kind of thud a large orange sandbag would make if sandbags had fur. "While you're down there," said the Word Detective, "see if you can find me a time machine. Without one of those, I think we may just be out of luck. This is one tough nut to crack.

"The only theory I've heard that even comes close," he continued, as the cat pulled himself up from the floor, "is the one about the early Dutch settlers around New York calling the English *Jan Kees,* or *John Cheese,* their idea of an deadly insult. Go figure. I guess you had to be there."

The cat looked puzzled, then asked, "But how did we get from the Dutch calling the British *John Cheese* to the Brits calling the colonists *yankees?*" With a look of quiet determination, the Word Detective rose from his desk and headed toward the door. "That's what I aim to nail down right now, bucko," he said, glancing around the office, "just as soon as I find my hat."

zarf

The large orange cat sat alone in the Word Detective's office, staring contemplatively out the window and pondering the vagaries of language, the mysteries of history, and the eternal question of dinner. A tuna melt from the deli downstairs would be nice, he decided as he waddled toward the telephone. He hoped the Detective's credit was still good.

The phone rang just as he reached it, and the cat kicked the receiver from its cradle on the fourth ring as he had been taught. "Hello," he announced in his best BBC accent, "You have reached the offices of the Word Detective. We can't come to the phone right now. Please leave a message after the beep. *Beeeeep.*" He hoped the caller hadn't noticed the slight belch in the middle of his *beeeeep*.

"Hello?" a voice ventured, "Word Detective? This is your editor at Algonquin. Listen, we really like the entry for *Yankee*, but we can't end the book without a *z* word. Readers will think

EVAN MORRIS

there are pages missing. Take your time and see what you can do before tomorrow, O.K.?"

Carpe diem, thought the cat. This might be his shot at the big time. "Hi, this is the Word Detective's assistant," he said, quickly dropping the accent. "I'm afraid Mister Detective went to the post office and won't be back for at least a month. Maybe I can help. How about *zarf*—you know, those little plastic cup holders you find next to the coffee machines in offices?"

"*Zarf?*" said the Editor skeptically. "Is that a real word? Sounds like something a dachshund would say. And by the way, since when does Mister Word Snoop have an assistant? He told me he was a hermit living in a tree house."

"He exaggerates a little for tax purposes," the cat explained. "Of course *zarf* is a real word. The word *zarf* itself is Arabic for 'container,' and zarfs are commonly used in the Middle East to hold porcelain coffee cups. Saves the pinkies from scorching, you see. Middle Eastern zarfs, however, are usually made of metal, often in very ornate designs, and sometimes, if the owner is both wealthy and very fond of coffee, the zarf is made of gold or silver and inlaid with jewels. *Zarf* first appeared in English in the mid-nineteenth century."

"No kidding," the Editor said. "So I'm actually using a zarf right now. How come mine doesn't have any jewels on it?"

"Maybe that wretched office coffee you're drinking dissolved them," snapped the cat, starting to feel dizzy from hunger. "What can I say? The world has gone to the dogs. Hey, I gotta go now. I've got a date with a tuna."

"Somehow," said the Editor, "that doesn't surprise me at all. Well, if Mister Snoop ever gets back, tell him the book is done. All we need now is an author photo for the book jacket."

"No problem," said the cat, glancing around the room. His gaze settled on the Word Detective's latest addition to the deranged decor of the office, a faded FBI wanted poster seeking the apprehension of a fugitive embezzler. "I'll have it to you first thing in the morning."

We can't end the book without a Z word.

There are literally hundreds of books and Internet sites to-day that provide useful information about English word origins, far too many to list in this limited space. What follows, therefore, should be considered merely a starting point for readers interested in pursuing the subject.

The big enchilada and sine qua non in the field of English etymology is, of course, *The Oxford English Dictionary, Second Edition* (Oxford: Oxford University Press, 1989), which currently is available in four forms: the twenty-volume full edition, the single-volume compact edition (which uses microscopic type to squeeze nine pages of the full edition onto each page and comes with a very nice magnifier), the CD-ROM edition, and online, at www.oed.com. If you own a computer, I strongly recommend the CD-ROM edition of the *OED,* as it makes searching for information a snap and is thus much easier to use than either hard-copy edition or the Internet edition.

Other reference works that cover a variety of word origins include those on the following list. The authors whose works are listed here, incidentally, can be considered "sure bets"—any other titles you happen across by the same authors are sure to be worth your while.

Algeo, John, ed. *Fifty Years Among the New Words.*
Cambridge: Cambridge University Press, 1991.

Allen, Irving Lewis. *The City in Slang: New York Life and Popular Speech.* New York: Oxford University Press, 1993.

Ammer, Christine. *Have a Nice Day — No Problem!: A Dictionary of Clichés.* New York: Penguin Books USA, 1992.

Ammer, Christine. *It's Raining Cats and Dogs — and Other Beastly Expressions.* St. Paul: Paragon House, 1989.

Ayto, John. *Twentieth Century Words.* Oxford: Oxford University Press, 1999.

Ayto, John. *Dictionary of Word Origins.* Boston: Little, Brown, 1990.

Barnhart, David K., and Allan A. Metcalf. *America in So Many Words: Words That Have Shaped America.* Boston: Houghton Mifflin, 1997.

Barnhart, Robert K. *The Barnhart Concise Dictionary of Etymology.* New York: HarperCollins Publishers, 1995.

Bryson, Bill. *Made in America: An Informal History of the English Language in the United States.* New York: William Morrow, 1994.

Cassidy, Frederic G., ed. *Dictionary of American Regional English.* 3 vols. Cambridge: Harvard University Press, 1985–96. Further volumes forthcoming.

Chapman, Robert L. *Dictionary of American Slang*. 3rd ed. New York: HarperCollins Publishers, 1995.

Dalzell, Tom. *Flappers 2 Rappers: American Youth Slang*. Springfield, Mass.: Merriam-Webster, 1996.

Dickson, Paul. *Slang*. New York: Pocket Books, 1998.

Farmer, J. S., and W. E. Henley. *Slang and Its Analogues*. 7 vols. London and Edinburgh: n.p., 1890–1904.

Green, Jonathon, *Slang Down the Ages*. London: Kyle Cathie, 1993.

Lighter, J. E., ed. *Random House Historical Dictionary of American Slang*. 2 vols. New York: Random House, 1994–97. Further volumes forthcoming.

Mencken, H. L. *The American Language*. 4th ed. New York: Alfred A. Knopf, 1976.

Morris, William, and Mary D. Morris. *Morris Dictionary of Word and Phrase Origins*. 2nd ed. New York: Harper-Collins Publishers, 1988.

Partridge, Eric. *A Dictionary of Catch Phrases*. Briarcliff Manor, N.Y.: Stein and Day, 1977.

Partridge, Eric. *A Dictionary of Slang and Unconventional English*. 8th ed. New York: Macmillan Publishing, 1984.

Rawson, Hugh. *Devious Derivations*. New York: Crown Publishers, 1994.

Rawson, Hugh. *Rawson's Dictionary of Euphemisms and Other Doubletalk.* New York: Crown Publishers, 1995.

Rawson, Hugh. *Wicked Words.* New York: Crown Publishers, 1989.

Rees, Nigel. *Phrases and Sayings.* London: Bloomsbury Publishing, 1995.

Rosten, Leo. *The Joys of Yiddish.* New York: McGraw-Hill, 1968.

Wentworth, Harold, and Stuart Berg Flexner. *Dictionary of American Slang.* New York: Thomas Y. Crowell, 1975.

A side from the *Word Detective* Web site (www.word-detective.com), there are an ever-increasing number of excellent Web sites devoted to words and language. Here is a small sampling of some of the excellent sites out there:

American Dialect Society (www.americandialect.org): The ADS is a scholarly organization that studies the English language in North America and produces the journal *American Speech*. On the ADS Web site, you can read back issues of the ADS newsletter, subscribe to the ADS-L e-mail discussion list, search the ADS-L archives, and, of course, join the ADS.

World Wide Words (www.quinion.com/words): A fascinating site from the United Kingdom, regularly updated. Michael Quinion has written a marvelous series of short essays on topics ranging from *mondegreens* to Polari, a language spoken only in the British theater.

Random Word of the Day (www.randomhouse.com/jesse/index.cgi): This site, developed by former Random House senior editor Jesse Sheidlower, used to be known as Jesse's Word of the Day. Jesse has since gone on to become North American editor of the *Oxford English Dictionary*, but this site, now staffed by a tag team of Random House editors, still answers language questions from readers with wit, style, and solid scholarship.

Dave Wilton's Etymology Page (www.wilton.net/etyma1.htm): An excellent site that includes a very well written and concise history of the English language as well as a fascinating exploration of the most common errors people make when trying to figure out the origins of English words. You'll also find an alphabetical index to explanations of the real origins of scores of words and phrases.

Wordplay (www.wolinskyweb.com/word.htm): A site offering dozens of links to other sites that feature "fun with words." Judi Wolinsky, the author of this page, has done an excellent job of assembling these links and updates her list frequently.